A REVOLUTIONARY SOLDIER

REVISED AND PREPARED

BY

JOHN M. ROBERTS

AYER COMPANY PUBLISHERS, INC.
NORTH STRATFORD, NH 03590

Reprint Edition, 2002
Ayer Company Publishers, Inc.
Ayer Road
North Stratford, NH 03590

Reprint Edition, 1980
Arno Press Inc.

———

Editorial Supervision: RITA LAWN
Reprinted from a copy in the State Historical Society of Wisconsin Library

AMERICAN MILITARY EXPERIENCE
ISBN for complete set: 0-405-11850-3
See last pages of this volume for titles.

Manufactured in the United States of America

———

Library of Congress Cataloging in Publication Data

Collins, James Potter, 1763-1844.
   Autobiography of a Revolutionary soldier.

   (American military experience)
   Reprint of the 1859 ed. published by Feliciana
Democrat, Clinton, La.
   1. Collins, James Patter, 1763-1844. 2. United
States—History—Revolution, 1775-1783—Secret service.
3. Spies—United States—Biography. 4. North Carolina
—Militia—Biography. I. Roberts, John M.
II. Title. III. Title: A Revolutionary soldier.
IV. Series.
E280.C64A32   1979   973.3'3'0924 [B]   78-22378
ISBN 0-405-11855-4

AUTOBIOGRAPHY
OF
A REVOLUTIONARY SOLDIER

THE AMERICAN MILITARY EXPERIENCE

Advisory Editor
Richard H. Kohn

Editorial Board
Bernard Brodie
Edward M. Coffman
Morris Janowitz
Russell F. Weigley

*See last pages of this volume
for a complete list of titles.*

A REVOLUTIONARY SOLDIER

REVISED AND PREPARED

BY

JOHN M. ROBERTS, Esq.

CLINTON, LA.,
FELICIANA DEMOCRAT, PRINT,
1859.

ENTERED. according to the Act of Congress, in the year 1859, by JOHN M. ROBERTS, ESQR., in the Clerk's Office of the United States District Court of the State of Louisiana.

COMPTROLLER'S DEPARTMENT,
RALEIGH, N. C., Jan. 30, 1858.

DEAR SIR—Your letter, requesting me to examine the Records in my Office, for evidence of the payments made to JAMES COLLINS, a soldier of the Revolutionary war, was duly received.

On a full and thorough examination of the Records, I find sundry payments made to JAMES COLLINS, in the Halifax, Wilmington. Salisbury, and Morgan Districts.

Very respectfully, your obedient servant,

(Signed)   C. H. BROGDEN, Comptroller.

To JOHN M. ROBERTS, ESQ., Clinton, La.

To the Children

OF

JAMES P. COLLINS, Deceased.

THE PRESENT WORK,

IS RESPECTFULLY DEDICATED,

BY JOHN M. ROBERTS.

CLINTON, LA.

INDEX.

		PAGE
PREFACE		iii
CHAPTER		
I.	Early days and ancestry,	11
II.	Trouble among the Tories,	22
III.	Minute men,	28
IV.	Skirmish with the enemy,	39
V.	Scouting,	45
VI.	Battle of King's Mountain,	49
VII.	Battle of the Cowpens,	55
VIII.	A hazardous adventure,	59
IX	Ferretting out Tories,	65
X.	Return home,	68
XI.	Various occupations,	73
XII.	Scenes and adventures,	78
XIII.	The Spring of 1791. The Indians,	82
XIV.	Religious views. Dancing and singing schools. Hunting,	90
XV.	"The days when I went courting,"	98
XVI.	Visit to my father. Return to Georgia. Marriage,	109
XVII.	Boy attacked by Indians. Drunkenness. Spell of fever,	118
XVIII.	Return to business. Death of my wife. Second marriage,	125
XIX.	Horse purchase. A strange disease,	138
XX.	Visit to a celebrated doctor. New and strange religious sect,	148
XXI.	Preaches a sermon. Mysterious cure,	154
XXII.	Visit to Tennessee. Encounter with Indians,	162
XXIII.	Removal to Tennessee. Last Remarks,	169

PREFACE.

The publisher offers the present work, not with a view through vanity, of adding to the catalogue of historical information of the brave and patriotic sires of the revolution—not that he expects to receive a larger amount of applause, than those who have already filled the minds of the country with a brilliant rehearsal of their illustrious deeds of heroism, and in fact, whose merits have not yet been half told, and which is fervently hoped will continue to be repeated in strains of enthusiasm, as long as a solitary vestige of republicanism is left to linger in the American heart. No, he feels that it is incumbent on him to make a disclosure as a child of this republic, when in his power so to do, of all the acts and deeds of those whose lives were tried in defence of the great cause of liberty, happiness and peace of this, now, mighty and grand republic, even though these words should come from an humble soldier. It is asserted, by some, that there is a sufficient amount of historical knowledge already given : *any more would be superfluous.* This kind of reasoning is certainly poor and worthless. Are there too many memoir authorities to sustain the glorious principles of christianity and religious truth? Certainly not, will be answered by the friends of its progress. We take it then, that principles of freedom, of republicanism, of brotherly union and national enfranchisement, are some of the forced and legitimate results issuing alone from the word of inspiration, and are intimately blended and inseparably interwoven with the Bible. The man who is unfriendly to one, is surely a stranger to the other; and there are certainly no grounds for compromise. Besides, what can more easily quiet the turbulent and boisterous passions of an angry mind, than to dispel by force of reason, to drive away the dark and benighted clouds of ignorance, that the rays of intelligence may shed soft and congenial influences in the heart, awakening into being different thoughts and different feelings. To stand aloof and not participate in these sentiments, is surely depriving ones-self of all the real enjoyments of life.

The present work is written in an unpolished and plain style; but it is written in the words of truth. It is written by a soldier who stood in the front of the many battles of the enemy—whose life was exposed to whatever danger that should be necessarily encountered, both by night and by day, undergoing fatigue of all kinds. The latter part of this work contains more of the history of his life in a private capacity, than of the fields of battle, and his only characteristic as a man of boldness of sentiments and "truth unvarnished."

There are facts, in the present work, in regard to the battle of the King's Mountain—which former historians have not altogether taken so much notice—which goes to show the actual situation of the scattering and small troops of Col. Moffit, their difficulties and struggles with the home enemies at that time (i. e., the Tories) being compelled to rely almost entirely upon their own resources, or in fact, absolutely having no prospect of future reward from the public, the majority being very poor and unable to obtain the necessary means suited to the field of battle. But these embarrassments did not baffle their designs, for they were determined to conquer or lose their lives in the contest. They were contending for freedom, for liberty and for the prosperity of a new republic, that America should be the home of social and national happiness, and it is presumed that no one will doubt but that their efforts have been crowned with triumphant success.

It may appear strange to the reader that the author of the present narrative closes his memoirs so suddenly and apparently unfinished. It is doubtless that he did not more than half finish his design, for he moved and lived in the State of Louisiana quite a number of years after the time that his autobiography closed, having reared a number of children, whom even now, may be living in this State; but at the time of his undertaking the present work, he was of extreme age and nearly blind. Not to boast of the merits of our old, and now nearly all deceased, sires of the revolution, beggars a proper want of knowledge as well as a proper want of a pure principle of patriotism in our hearts.

Everything that we may claim as a happy republic, is alone through the bold and vigorous exertions of those brave and gallant men, their trials and undertakings, as well as all the fatigues of war. They were guided by the spirit of freedom and happiness. The atmosphere they inhaled, inspired them with a love of freedom; the pure water they drank from the pebbly rivulets, stimulated them; the evergreen shade, the fertile soil enchanted them by their magic charms to industry; while an indomitable disposition not to be fettered in the chains of despotism, awoke them to a double energy that has never been equalled in the annals of the world. Yes, reader, this old and venerable father of the revolution died before he had completed his own story; but his "handwriting is on the wall," and brings fresh and living associations of the loveliest character to our hearts—it calls as with a "bugle blast" to our recollection, the perilous condition that awaited moral, religious and civil liberty. To undertake to describe the boasted wealth and honor of the American republic, in comparison with any other nation now on the globe, would be extreme vanity; but we cannot charge our minds with too much veneration for the character of our past and deceased fathers of the revolution, however simple and plain may have been their manner and style of speaking and writing, or however rough and seemingly unpolished their habits and manners in comparison with the present age of wealth and luxury, for like Napoleon, they had no friend but their sword, yet the same untiring, immortal, unalterable disposition to implant the true and genuine principles of social and national happiness inspired their souls to deeds of noble daring and the "pæan notes of liberty" clang to them as the dreams of the Messiah Ben David does to the Wandering Jew to this day. They beheld by faith the star of freedom in the distance. They beheld, the Star of Bethlehem by inspiration whose cheering beams they fervently hoped would shoot athwart the else rayless void of more than midnight gloom. Yes, yes,—the gentle dove that rested on Mount Olivet, was not a stranger to their hearts' feelings, although deluged in blood and carnage and yet they hoped to see the gentle messenger return with the olive branch of peace—not that they felt like surrendering the love of country, but to accomplish a far more rational deed—a deed of universal enfranchisement—to establish an asylum for the oppressed of every nation, where the altars of religion, the temples of justice and the free and actual happiness of man could rest undisturbed and man should gain his living "by the sweat of his brow." These were the sentiments of our old forefathers; they loved their country, for it is natural and should be so; for everything like prosperity depends on that one sacred tie. Hear the words of a gentleman of this State, on the same subject, in a public address. I here quote as I think them appropriate to the present theme: "Love of country seems to be an universal principle. Even the inhabitant of the ice-bound and frozen regions of Greenland regard it as the best country upon which the sun ever shone.

Should we compare then, ourselves to any nation on earth at the present time? If the history of our country; if the benign blessings which our glorious institutions shed like dews from heaven upon each and every one of our citizens; if a love and veneration of the tombs of our fathers, the memory of Washington and his time-honored compatriots and the sweet name of America itself; if these are not sufficient to inspire one of Columbia's sons with emotions of patriotism, he is too far lost for salvation to reach him—too detestable to dwell in the habitations of man, and should be driven with eternal infamy from the face of the earth, banished to the dreary rock of Patmos, or some solitary isle of the ocean, uninhabited by mortal man, and unfrequented, save by loathsome vultures which are drawn thither to feed and gloat themselves upon the putrescent substances which old ocean, in the mighty expurgating commotion of her waters, indignantly heaves from her surface. No American, I repeat, need be advised of his duty as a patriot and lover of his country: the scenes enacted on the battle-fields of Yorktown, King's Mountain, the Plains of Chalmette, the heights of Cerro Gordo are sufficient."

This is one side of the picture and it is fervently hoped to be a correct one; but let us examine the matter a momemt by way of premise: First. who would deny that it was the duty of the parent to give and render all the care in the bounds of reason, and even sometimes overleap this mark to protect their offspring? Again, it must be admitted that it is the duty of the parent to admonish and devise the best and most wholesome comfort to the health and happiness of their offspring; place before them the best advice, moral and religious, as well as inculcate the feelings of love to country, kindred and friends, to have the mind properly prepared to enter into the various scenes and occupations of life, fulfilling in every sense the sacred word of the old book of the Bible, "Raise up a child in the way he should go and when he gets old he will not depart from it." So great was this principle once inculcated in the laws of some of the Oriental nations, that if the child was not educated for some ostensible occupation in life, the parent was subject to the greatest penalty, and prevented from being recognized on a par with the same advantages of other citizens, and sometimes almost the forfeiture of life, so great has this one principle been adhered to; so great has this point been carried in the Divine Law of our Heavenly Father towards the happiness and salvation of sin-atoning man, that he gave his "only begotten Son" to ransom by a vicarious death on the rugged cross, as an expiation of the guilt of man; thereby setting an example of parental fidelity to man. God has by holy decree indelibly stamped this cardinal feature in all animal creation, from man, who was formed after his own image and likeness, to the lowest of the beast creation. No opinion of man can set aside the "Law of God," and it is to be regretted as a lamentable error in the faculty of man to seek any means to contradict these rules.

Second—It is for the purpose of perpetuating natural kindness and brotherly union that the "golden rule of charity" was pronounced with so much emphasis in the expressions of the Apostle Paul in his writings to the first Corinthians, in his chapter thirteenth, and particularly in his first verse, he remarks: "Though I speak with the tongues of men and angels and have not charity. I am become as sounding brass or a tinkling cymbal." (Please read this chapter.)

Now let us turn and contemplate the reciprocal affections that should be manifested from the offspring to the natural parent. and let us apply these rules to our natural, national, moral and civil conditions in life: First—Is it natural for the child to love the parent to which it owes all its protection and care, being entirely weak and destitute of all power of self-protection?

Second—Why should these principles be applied in a national sense? In the great volume of universal love the language bursts forth in strains too eloquent and apprises man of the truth. Not to love home—the place from which he first inhaled his breath of existence—not to love the numerous fond and endearing associations of youthful recollections—the little stream, the tall tree, the old fence overgrown with the briar—where the wild bird builds her annual nest; the mother's smile and the father's stern advice, the old schoolhouse, the college wall, the youthful girl with sweet and innocent caress, the friend's warm hand, the prayer, the song, the "dance of fearless, thoughtless joy"—can these be erased from the human heart? Methinks not.

Third—The moral condition that may exist, brings a different tide of feeling, and places man under a different position in life.

Fourth—The civil or social state. In this character man stands amenable and quite responsible to the power above him as well as to the earthly power equal with him. The responsibility he owes to his fellow man in this world, is the highest consideration he can contemplate; to forget this, man forgets the link of chain by which he is bound, he becomes a drone and dies as he lived: fashion, pomp and wealth are buried with him. This theme is worthy of our serious reflection; to comment would be but to strain the mind and lead to endless disclosures and mere waste of time. Let us again ask, why should there be a dereliction of duty on man to continue an unceasing devotion to country, home and friends? Is it for the purpose of personal gain? This question requires some investigation. 1. There are reasons that may induce a man (as I may say) to leave or forsake the early idols of his heart, youthful affections, and all the circumstances that surround his happiness or his interest—condition in this life. 2. Oppressive control, ungenerous and predominant suasion, the cruel exercise of self-will and regardless management are some causes, perhaps the hope of health is one: these are plain reasons, under qualified circumstances. Now let us ask ourselves—Is the love of honor, love of ambition, and unrestrained power, and self-sacrifice a cause sufficient to erase those earth-born principles and national fidelity. Is it the love of mammon or sordid gold a useless ornament to the miser who cannot take one cent with him when the last duty is required of him, (that is to die, leaving all his earthly hoardings here behind him?) Is it for the sake of health? Let him remember that all mankind are subjected alike to the same dispensations of Divine Providence. It is a lifeless subterfuge and weighs not a fraction in the scale of reason. Let us, as a nation apply the foregoing questions to our own hearts. Have we by wealth and almost unrestrained power forgotten "the Rock whence ye are hewn, and the hole of the pit whence ye are digged?" Are the memorable days that have been celebrated as typical of our national independence such as the Fourth of July, Washington's birthday and the Eighth of January beginning to fall back into the shades of forgetfulness? Is the nation engulphed in a political mania, or is it mammon or ostensible wealth, false show, that causes us to turn a deaf ear to those memorable and early scenes? It is to be hoped that the foregoing hints will be sufficient and duly appreciated.

Yes, our venerable father of the revolution, died in his eighty-first year, in the State of Texas, after "running the race that was set before him," after enjoying immeasurable happiness and devotional thankfulness, and submissive feeling of adoration for the mercies and blessings of that omnipotent God who crowned the efforts of his life in establishing "peace on earth and good will to men." He died as he lived, resigned to his fate—he died without a murmur, composed, serene—his body was consigned to the dust, and his soul to bloom in an undying immortality. Our venerable patriarch was known to be a man of exceedingly industrious habits, was always engaged in some enterprise or business—he threw away but a few hours, believing it a great error in man to while away the hours of his life in idleness and frivolity—" that Satan doth still mischief find for idle hands to do." Thus, we may ascribe as one reason for his longevity. He was small in stature ; he had but little sickness in comparison to other persons ; he possessed robust health ; he was also a very neat person in his dress ; easy and polite in his manners ; filled with good humor and jokes, and was very fond of company at times ; his manners were nevertheless grave and dignified. He made it a rule not to be forward in breaking conversation, rather reserved ; yet you could see the fire of wit kindling in his eye, which is said to be the unerring index that declares the power of the soul that sits enthroned within. He was kind and generous to a fault—the chamber of the sick, the pillow of the dying, the vigils of the dead, never missed his sympathy and kind attention ; administering on all occasions whatever services he could render. Many will long remember him for it, for if there is a sentiment in the human heart that truly indicates a noble, God-like spirit, a spirit of a great and generous soul, filled to the last expansion with patriotism and philanthrophy, it is to visit our poor and afflicted humanity in hours of sickness and want. Our old friend was universally respected by all who knew him, and greatly beloved by those who were intimately acquainted with him. As a husband--as a father—in those attributes the time honored and lasting recollections cling, if possible, closer than the bark to the tree, to the bosom of his family ; for like the lofty tree which lifts its umbrageous head towards Heaven, basking in the free air in majestic grandeur, where thousands take repose and exult beneath its refreshing shade, so did our venerable friend stand among the children of men, " that no power could break or favor bend "—one straight and onward way in life—always observing truth and punctuality as the polar star and sheet-anchor to direct and maintain his course ; for he was never known to fall behind, if possible, with his obligations to his fellow men. This was his tried character. His accumulations of wealth were comparatively small, but he always strove to have a sufficiency to meet the necessary wants of a respectable life, and enjoyed it to the full fruition. His doors were thrown open to distress, and the hand of charity extended, wherever he thought it really necessary. He was remarkable for his frankness of expression, and candid in the transactions of business. He was a man who had not all the early opportunities of what is termed a liberal education, but he devoted in the latter part of his life, considerable of his time to reading, especially the Bible, and seemed to reflect a great deal on its holy pages. His opinions were received in all matters, when consulted ; he had few enemies which caused his opinions to go farther than perhaps the most of men, as he was not meddlesome with other people's affairs. He was not quarrelsome, but at times, we suppose, from the many early conflicts with the enemies of his country, became excited at the mention of the revolutionary war, especially at the mention of the name of Tory, for he had an undying hatred for them which sometimes caused him to betray the weakness of his feelings, and would become transported by that monster which he termed his greatest self-enemy. We consider it to be almost universally the case in those whose temperaments are naturally given to excitement, and who have had to go through sanguinary scenes, and have come off victorious, to give way at times to exuberance of passion ; but they were soon over with him, provided the object of his indignation was removed immediately, otherwise, battle to the hilt. As observed, he devoted a great deal of his time in his old age to reading, and among other works, were those containing descriptions of the battles of the revolution, and among them were those in which he was engaged. He thought that their description was not sufficiently elaborate, which brought him to the conclusion to write a narrative of his own life and adventures. The relative position he stood in as a spy, in the beginning of the war, and as a soldier at its conclusion, he thought it "might not be amiss" to add a few words in his way, to the world, and to the rising generation. We believe that it is a natural instinct in the bosom of all men, who have passed through similar trials—as our venerable father did—to tell all about it as far as possible ; and it is right that we should listen to their stories with care and attention. In this we show respect to them as well as gratitude on our part. This light which he has left, is fervently hoped to burn forever in the heart of every true lover of liberty : it is his tribute that he owes to his country—come and get it.

AUTOBIOGRAPHY
OF
A REVOLUTIONARY SOLDIER:

CHAPTER I.

EARLY DAYS AND ANCESTRY.

" Praise to the warriors, who fought and who bled
In Liberty's battles. Praise ! Praise to the dead.
Bind on the brows of the living, though hoary,
A chaplet of laurels they merit so well,
And sing to the dead one loud anthem of glory.
Loud, louder, yet louder, their proud notes shall swell."

IN REFLECTING on past events, and comparing them with the present, and having arrived at that period of life which unfits me for the more active employments and busy pursuits that have hitherto occupied my time, I thought it might not be amiss to amuse myself by writing a few incidents of my life, although they may not be interesting to any one (who may chance to read these pages), yet might be, in some instances, amusing as well as important to some of my progeny when I am no more. In writing the incidents of my past life, I am forced to depend entirely upon memory; by moving from one place to another, and meeting with sundry accidents, I lost all the important papers and notes which I could apply to as references, and can therefore give but an incomplete and unfinished idea of many things.

Before I proceed farther, it will perhaps be necessary to say something of my parentage, of which I can detail but little, being only in possession of some statements given to me by my father, after I became of an age to listen, and hear him recite, the most interesting stories about our ancestors and familiy. I learned from him, that my grand-father, Charles Collins, resided in the city of Waterford, in Ireland, a man of considerable wealth; my grand-mother Susannah was of a noted family of the Radcliffes. Their family consisted of seven sons and one daughter; the sons were, John, James, Edward, Charles, Josiah, Alexander, and Daniel. My grandfather, after giving his sons a liberal education, settled them in some professional business; but what particular occupations or business I am unable to say, except that the two eldest sons, John and James, were put in command of two ships engaged in the African slave-trade. My father, Daniel, the youngest son, was continued at school, and my grandfather about that time dying, my father was left under the control of his mother, who continued him at school until he completed his education, as far as was intended. He being of a restless disposition, became dissatisfied with his mother's plans respecting his future course of life; every proposition he made to his mother was discountenanced and absolutely rejected, and she on the other hand, being of a resolute and determined mind, forced him to obedience contrary to his will. His mother, however, furnished him with a sufficient amount of money necessary for his expenses on all occasions, requiring at the same time, a strict account of the manner in which it was expended. While matters were in this state between them, he determined to leave his country and sail for America. This design he had to keep a profound secret, for if his plans were discovered by his mother, immediate steps would be taken to prevent his leaving. He found an opportunity of conferring with the captain of a vessel, then bound for America—perhaps for the sake of getting some money. The captain agreed to favor his plans, and also assisted him in devising schemes to obtain the requisite amount of funds from his mother. Success favored his plans, and all things were arranged satisfactorily, for my father. When the ship was ready to sail, he was conveyed on board without the knowledge, or even suspicion, of any of his friends, and accordingly sailed for America. The exact age of my father at that time, I am unable, positively to give, because I am without dates, and can only guess from subsequent events: at all events it was while he was under control of his mother, and not authorized to manage his own affairs. He landed at Philadelphia, and there got into some temporary business, being a good penman and calculator, for I believe I can say, without being in error, he was one of the first class of penman I have ever met with; he was so considered, at least, by those who professed to be good judges, besides which he stood in the first class in arithmetic. He next undertook to teach an English school in the country, near Philadelphia, and continued in that business until the commencement of what was called the French and Indian war. He then quit his school and joined the army—I think according to his statement to me, this was in 1754. He continued in the army until some time in the winter after Braddock was defeated, and his time of service expiring, he quit the army and returned to Philadelphia, when some short time after he married my mother; this was early in the winter of 1756. He again resumed his former occupation of school-teaching, out in the country, where he continued about five years. People were at that time emigrating to the South'; but before I proceed further, I must here mention a circumstance which occurred one day while my father was at his school. The house caught fire, and my mother with difficulty, saved her children, while the house and every article in it were consumed.

My father, in order to secure land on which to support a

family that appeared to be increasing, determined to look in the South for the object, and immediately set out in the spring of 1763. in order to view the country. In the fall of the same year, perhaps in the month of October, he started with his family for his place of destination, and had arrived within four miles of it when he stopped at the house of a Mr. Jourdan. In the morning, my mother was unable to proceed, and the good man furnished my father with a house, or rather a cabin, in which to shelter the family from the weather, at which place my mother brought me forth on the 22d November. Thus was I born by the way and have been a wayfaring man ever since. My father proceeded to build some kind of shelter, and improve the land on which he had determined to settle, and move his family, so soon as my mother's situation admitted. The place was then supposed to be within the limits of North Carolina and then called Tryon County, and my father was appointed Clerk of the first court that was ever held in the county, called Tryon Court; but afterwards, when the boundary of the State was ascertained, it fell about four miles in the State of South Carolina, in what was called York County, or District. Of my mother I have but a very imperfect recollection; however, as well as I can remember the statement given me, her parents had lmigrated from Ireland previous to the time that my father came over and settled in Philadelphia. Her name was Elizabeth Heland; she was a small woman and of a delicate constitution, and old women, who were her neighbors; have since spoken of her to me in highly flattering terms. She lived to have seven children, of which I was the fourth; three sons and four daughters. She died a few days after the birth of her seventh child, and it died a few days after her. My father was then left with six children, all young. I was about three years old. Some of the neighboring women took three of my sisters, and my father retained his sons at home, I being one of that number. Occasionally, a neighboring woman, who had no children, would take me with her and keep me sometime. My father continued to stay at home and keep house, after some manner, I know not how, for perhaps about fourteen months, when he married a young widow, with one child; who, after marriage with my father, had thirteen children. I recollect to have eaten at my father's table, when fifteen of his children, all grown, and mostly all heads of families, sat at the same table. It was my father's practice to be engaged in teaching every winter season and working on his farm during the summer; so soon as the marriage with his second wife took place I was put at school. During the summer season, the schoolhouse was always occupied by some other teacher, but was invariably reserved for my father during the winter. In summer, I was only sent to school at intervals, as I could not be spared out of the farm, for I was put to ploughing before I could turn the plough at the end of the land.

My father was rigid in his discipline, both at school and at home, and every rule that he laid down, must be strictly complied with, or on failure, punishment was the inevitable consequence, and I often thought he used more severity towards me than necessary, in order to make me an example for others. So it was, I was continued at school, sometimes under his tuition and sometimes under that of other teachers, until I was about twelve years old; but, by the way, I always got more indulgence when under the control of any other teacher, than of my father.

My father was also a man of strict morals and never admitted any immoral conversation or conduct in his presence, or otherwise; if the same was reported to him, he would punish the offender. He was also a strict observer of the Sabbath day, consequently he enjoined it on all his family to attend to religious duties, and on that day the Bible must be read, and every Sunday evening a certain portion must be committed to memory and rehearsed under his inspection, together with the Lord's Prayer, and what is called the Larger and

Shorter Catechism. There was no fishing, shooting, hunting or visiting permitted on that day, or trading or dealing of any kind whatever, nor was it fashionable in the neighborhood. I omitted to mention in the proper place, that agreeable to the rules of the Church to which my father belonged, all children were presented to the Church when young, for baptism. Accordingly I was presented and was baptized by a clergyman, to whom my father was somewhat partial, named James Potter, after whom I was called; hence the name, J. P.

But to return to my subject—when I was about twelve years of age, I had learned to read English pretty well and write a fair hand, and gained a tolerable knowledge of arithmetic and my father proposed sending me to college, in order to prepare me for studying divinity, but I, not feeling a willingness, objected and my father being somewhat straitened in circumstances on account of an increasing family, determined I should engage in some mechanical occupation, and proposed binding me to a tailor. I objected to that also, and suggested that I would rather work in wood, but he took his own way in the matter and bound me to a tailor by the name of McMavey, for the term of five years. It was stipulated in the contract that my father was to furnish all my necessary clothing, and that I should not, during my apprenticeship, be removed out of the State or county. The man to whom I was bound, was a man of very agreeable disposition, and remarkably good-humored, a good workman, very attentive to business, and of sober, industrious habits, so that I found myself placed in quite an agreeable situation. When I was placed under him, his family was small, having only a wife and one child, and another apprentice boy something older than myself, and who had been at work sometime. We then worked regularly in the shop; for my own part, I was put to some trifling business such as sewing up lining, &c. I had been at work about two months when Christmas came on—and here I must relate a little anecdote. The principal and his lady were invited to a party among their friends, and the other boy was permitted to go to his father's to spend the holidays, while it devolved on me to stay at home and keep house. There was nothing left me in charge to do, only to take care of the house. There was a large cat that generally lay about the fire. In order to try my mechanical powers, I concluded to make a suit of clothing for puss, and for my purpose gathered some scraps of cloth that lay about the shop-board, and went to work as hard as I could. Late in the evening I got my suit of clothes finished; I caught the cat, put on the whole suit—coat, vest and small-clothes—buttoned all on tight, and set down my cat to inspect the fit; unfortunately for me there was a hole through the floor close to the fireplace, just large enough for the cat to pass down; after making some efforts to get rid of the clothes, and failing, pussy descended through the hole and disappeared; the floor was tight and the house underpinned with brick, so there was no chance of pursuit. I consoled myself with a hope that the cat would extricate itself from its incumbrance, but not so; night came and I had made on a good fire and seated myself for some two or three hours after dark, when who should make their appearance but my master and mistress and two young men, all in good humor, with two or three bottles of rum. After all were seated around the fire, who should appear amongst us but the cat in his uniform. I was struck speechless, the secret was out and no chance of concealing; the cat was caught, the whole work inspected and the question asked, is this your day's work? I was obliged to answer in the affirmative; I would then have been willing to have taken a good whipping, and let it stop there, but no, to complete my mortification the clothes were carefully taken off the cat and hung up in the shop for the inspection of all customers that came in. I lived and went on very agreeably for two years and two months, when the revolutionary war began to make some interruption in the South, and the man with whom I lived took a notion to move high up in North Carolina, and as he was bound not to remove me, gave me up again to my father.

After returning home, the affairs of the country became more unsettled, and the people began to divide into parties. It was again proposed I should go to college. Accordingly arrangements were made and I was sent to Charlotte, in North Carolina. I had not remained there long until times became more troublesome, and I was again recalled home.

It was then customary for intinerant shoemakers to pass through the country and stop at the house of any farmer and make shoes for the family, and pass on to the next house where they were wanted. It was also a custom for every farmer to tan his own leather. It had been the practice of my father to have one of these shoemakers every winter, and his family increasing rapidly and he being somewhat straitened in circumstances, concluded to have me taught how to make shoes. Accordingly he agreed with an old man who set me to work, gave me some instructions, and I worked about three weeks, when I came home with some shoes as a sample of my performance. My father was a little hard to please and disliked the work, and truly it would not recommend itself. I gave as fair a statement as I could of the inattention to business, on the part of the old man, and it was determined that I should go to another. who it was thought, would be more attentive. The latter was a man who kept a shop, also, and was very industrious. There were two who worked at the business, and both took every pains they could to instruct me, and I soon made pretty smart improvement which pleased my father very much. With these two men I worked one winter season. I disliked the business and made great complaint to my father, and as he was inclined to industry and economy, he concluded he would put me to weaving. It was then the fashion for every family to manufacture every article of clothing that was worn, and the loom was occupied by the men while the females performed the spinning. Cotton was little used then—only as fillings, as it was called, for shirts, and clothing for females—while flax and wool composed the main materials for domestic clothing; as to broad cloth, it was but little used among the common people, and it was not uncommon for the son when grown up to become heir to his father's wedding coat, if his father had been able to procure broad cloth for that purpose.

It was concluded that I should learn to weave to save some expense in that way, and in the spring season I was put under the care of an Irish weaver to learn that business, where I continued during the summer. I was not averse to the weaving business and made considerable proficiency in the trade. I could then weave ten yards daily of what was called seven hundred linen. I had worked all this time for nothing, save information. Another weaver proposed to my father to give me wages. My father agreed and hired me to him; this man kept three looms and sometimes four in constant employ. I must here relate a little anecdote: I have mentioned before, that my father was rigid respecting Sunday, though not more so than some of his neighbors. I had no time to lose from the loom during the week, so one Sunday morning I concluded I must go home, some six or seven miles to get some clothing. My employer objected as it would be a breach of the Sabbath; I urged the necessity on the ground of losing no time in the week. He still stood opposed to the motion, threatening me with the vengeance of my father and utterly refusing his consent. While we were discussing the subject, a flock of sheep in a pasture fronting the door began to run and there appeared to be some confusion among them which drew the attention of the old man. A wolf had gotten among them, and before all hands could arrest his progress he had killed four, right in full view. The weaver then pleaded the right of necessity to skin the sheep and save his mutton, so I left him to save his meat and I went home to abide the consequences of my father's wrath on the subject. This, if I mistake not, was in the fall of 1779.

It was the custom in these times, for every farmer to make all the provisions he wanted for his use, viz.: corn, wheat, rye, barley, oats, pork, beef, and vegetables; also, potatoes, and whatever else was necessary; or, on failure, to pay his neighbor for whatever he might want, besides the risk of being called lazy, unless sickness or some misfortune occurred, in which case the neighbors were all very liberal to each other. Besides, if so disposed, he could keep liquor about his house, which was very general. He had his own malt, rye, corn, etc., prepared and ground at the mill, and taken to the still-house, where he received one gallon for every bushel of meal he delivered, or one half the quantity that the whole produced, took it home, stored it away in the cellar, and used it at pleasure. Here I must remark, that my father was very economical in his distribution, and reserved his whiskey for certain occasions. My step-mother's son and myself, being nearly the same age, were always together, when I was about home and would never divulge any thing on each other; my step-mother, by the way, was fully as great an economist as my father. We were both named James, and for distinction, I was often called Potter. We seldom got a dram more than once in the week and thought our rations rather small; we accordingly prepared us two small gourds, cleaned them out and converted them into bottles; they contained not more than half a pint each. In my father's absence we would keep a strict watch over the house, and when the old lady would disappear for the purpose of washing, or on some other business, which often happened. we would immediately repair to the house, open the hatch-way of the cellar, when one of us would descend and fill the two gourds, while the other would keep a good lookout for fear of being caught; we always came off clear without being suspected: our two gourds lasted us about three weeks or longer, for we used it very sparingly. At harvest time, or in gathering corn, it was a practice for every man to invite all the neighbors, male and famale, to assist in reaping, or husking his corn, for women thought it no hardship or disgrace, to labor in the fields; and some females, who stood high in society, were hard to beat, in the field, or at a corn heap. In the evening, or at night, when the labor was over, it generally wound up with a dance, and it was not rare to see women, more than forty years of age, cheerfully join in the same dance with the young. The old men who did not choose to dance, would sit by the fire, look on, and take their social glass of " over lively," and in the meantime, be sure to sing a few songs. The boys selected a place at a convenient distance from the house, kindled up a fire, and commenced running, jumping, and wrestling. They were always paired or matched by some of the larger class, chosen as judges. When the exercises were gone through, there came on a boxing match; any one that declined was declared a coward, yet some would stand it. For my own part, I disliked it, but was unwilling to own it, and determined to stand to the test. The rule was thus: A mark was made on the ground, the parties placed opposite, each with his toe to the mark, then a stick, handkerchief or rope was drawn between them and held by two of the judges. No man was to scratch, bite, gouge or strike in the eye; neither was he allowed to kick, but did the best he could, and hit to the best advantage so as to hurt his opponent. So soon as one gave back, the victory was proclaimed in favor of the other; this was all to be done in good humor, without any quarreling and if a fellow felt disposed to continue or was dissatisfied, he had to wait for the next time and get his remedy in the same way. Many of us went home pretty sore but never complained for fear of being punished by our parents. Some old men sanctioned the business, others were strongly opposed; among that number my father was one, and if ever he found out that I was in the boxing party, I was sure to get a *dressing* which hurt worse than all the boxing I ever was in.

CHAPTER II.

TROUBLE AMONG THE TORIES.

LET ME pass on. I began to grow up—times began to be troublesome, and people began to divide into parties. Those that had been good friends in times past, became enemies; they began to watch each other with jealous eyes, and were designated by the names of, Whig, and Tory. Recruiting officers were out in all directions, to enlist soldiers. My brother, older than myself, enlisted, and went off to the army. My father remonstrated against it but in vain. There was a Mr. Moffitt in the neighborhood who was then captain of the militia, was pretty shrewd and an active partizan. I had often been sent on business, by my father, in various directions through the country, and was frequently employed by others to hunt stray horses, &c., consequently I became acquainted with all the by-paths for twenty or thirty miles around. Moffitt consulted my father and it was agreed that I should be made use of merely as a collector of news. In order to prepare me for business, I had to receive several lectures. I was furnished with documents—sometimes a list of several stray horses with marks and brands, sometimes with papers and other business. I was to attend all public places, make no inquiry only about the business I was sent on, and pay strict attention to all that was passing in conversation and otherwise. I succeeded for some time without incurring the least suspicion, by which means the

Tories were several times disappointed in their plans without being able to account for the cause.

There existed at that time, at least three classes of Whigs, and three of Tories. The first class of Whigs were those who determined to fight it out to the last let the consequence be what it might; the second class were those who would fight a little when the wind was favorable, but so soon as it shifted to an unfavorable point would draw back and give up all for lost; the third class were those who were favorable to the cause, provided it prospered and they could enjoy the benefit but would not risk one hair of their heads to attain it.

There was a class of Tories who I believe were Tories from principle; another class believed it impossible for the cause of liberty to succeed, and thought in the end, whatever they got, they would be enabled to hold, and so become rich— they resorted to murdering and plunder, and every means to get hold of property; another class were Tories entirely through fear, and fit for nothing only to be made tools of by the others, and all cowards too.

There was another class of men amongst us, who pretended neutrality entirely on both sides; they pretended friendship to all, and prayed, "Good God!" "Good Devil!" not knowing into whose hands they might fall. Of these last there were several in the neighborhood, and by some means, some one or more became acquainted with the part I had acted; it became known to the Tories by the same means. They swore revenge. By some of the same people this was communicated to me, and I was cautioned of the danger that awaited me. It was also communicated to my father, and he advised me not to act in that part any longer, else I would suffer the penalty if caught. I took some alarm, and proposed enlisting in order to avoid danger. My father counseled me otherwise; he said the time was at hand when volunteers would be called for, and by joining them I would be equally safe; if I went to battle I stood as fair a chance ; besides, I would be less exposed, less fatigued, and if there should be any time of resting, I could come home and enjoy it ; he said he had had some experience and learned a lesson from that.

The British and Tories had overrun Georgia, and even driven out the celebrated Clarke, with all his veterans, as far as the very confines of North Carolina. All the south and south-western parts of South Carolina were nearly subjugated, and but a small part stood out with firmness, and that part itself divided. The British were pressing on Charleston, and had eventually got possession of it, and now began to come "squally times." So soon as Charleston fell, there was a proclamation for all to come forward, submit, and take protection ; peace and pardon should be granted. In order to expedite the business, there were officers sent out in various directions, with guards or companies of men, to receive the submission of the people. Vast numbers flocked in and submitted ; some through fear, some through willingness, and others, perhaps, through a hope that all things would settle down and war cease. But not so ; there was some conditions annexed, that some of the patriots of the day could not submit to and therefore determined to hold out a little longer. Among the officers sent out on this occasion, there was one Lord Hook, who came up and stationed himself at or near Fishing Creek at some distance below where we lived. His proclamation came out and a day was appointed to deliver his speeches. Almost all the men of families attended. He got up, harangued the people in a very rough and insulting manner and submitted his propositions for their acceptance. Some bowed to his sceptre, but far the greater part returned home without submitting.

I omitted to mention in the proper place, that in conversation with my father on the subject of enlistment, he observed to me that should volunteers be called which he confidently anticipated, that he would join the ranks ; he said, " though over age for the laws of my country to demand it, yet I think the nature of the case requires the best energies of every man who is a friend to liberty." Not many miles distant from where this Lord Hook, whom I have mentioned, had made his stand, there was a set of ironworks called Billy Hill's Ironworks, which were very profitable, both to the proprietor and all the country around. Lord Hook, provoked at the non-compliance of the people, determined to take vengeance; and to that end mustered his forces, charged on the ironworks, killed several men, set the works on fire, and reduced them to ashes. I must here relate the expression of my father, when he returned home from Lord Hook's exhibition. My step-mother asked him thus: "Well Daniel, what news?" My father replied, "Nothing very pleasant. I have come home determined to take my gun and when I lay it down, I lay down my life with it;" then turning to me said, "my son you may prepare for the worst; the thing is fairly at issue. We must submit and become slaves, or fight. For my part I am determined—to-morrow I will go and join Moffitt."

offitt, while these things were transpiring, had been engaged in raising volunteers, to be all mounted and ready at a minute's warning, to be called "Minute Men." He had already raised about seventy men. A nomination of officers had taken place, and he was unanimously chosen colonel of the troops. Accordingly, next day we shouldered our guns and went to Moffitt. The gun that I had to take was what was called a blue barrel shot gun. When we presented ourselves, "Well," said the colonel to my father, "Daniel, I suppose you intend to fight." My father said he had come to that conclusion. "Well, James," he said to me, "we shall have plenty for you to do, and two or three more such, if they could all have as good luck as you. We will try to take care of you and not let the Tories catch you."

In a few days there was a meeting of several officers, and it was determined to attack Lord Hook, and take vengeance for the burning of the ironworks. The time and place was appointed for a rendezvous, several parties united in the plan, we met, mounted on horseback, and advanced towards his lordship, early in the morning. Not long after sunrise, we came in sight of their headquarters, which were in a log building. In the rear of the building was a large peach orchard; at some distance behind the peach orchard we all dismounted and tied our horses; we then proceeded on foot through the orchard, thinking the peach trees would be a good safeguard, against the charge of the horseman. We had not proceeded far until the sentinels discovered us—fired on us and fled. The troops were soon mounted and paraded. This, I confess, was a very imposing sight, at least to me, for I had never seen a troop of British horse before, and thought they differed vastly in appearance from us—poor hunting-shirt fellows. The leader drew his sword, mounted his horse, and began to storm and rave, and advanced on us; but we kept close to the peach orchard. When they had got pretty near the peach trees, their leader called out, "disperse you d—d rebels, or I will put every man of you to the sword." Our rifle balls began to whistle among them, and in a few minutes my Lord Hook was shot off his horse and fell at full length; his sword flew out of his hand as he fell and lay at some distance, and both lay till some of his men gathered about him and around him two or three times. At lenght one halted and pointed his sword downward, seemed to pause a moment, then raising his sword, wheeled off and all started at full gallop. We then moved on to the house without opposition, but all had disappeared. In the yard sat two good looking fellows bleeding pretty freely, their horses standing at no great distance: one of whom was shot through the thigh.

Before the body of Hook was examined, two claimed the honor of killing him; both showed their guns and named the part of his body they had taken aim at, and both claimed the sword. One presented a large rifle, the other a very small one. The person having the small gun, cried, "I shot him! I shot him! I shot two balls which entered close under the ear." When Hook was examined, the two small balls were found to have passed through the place as described. We then bound up the wounds of the two men, took three swords, three brace of pistols, some powder and lead, perhaps my Lord Hook's watch, and but little else, and departed, every man for his own place. For my own part, I fired my old shot gun only twice in the action. I suppose I did no more harm than burning so much powder.

CHAPTER III.

MINUTE MEN.

THE ONLY man, in that section of country, who had raised or commanded Minute Men, was Moffitt. His ranks increased, in a short time, to number one hundred and twenty six, exclusive of our officers. The Tories became enraged at this deed of cruelty committed on their worthy friends, and swore revenge. In a short time we got the news that they were preparing to give us a blow, but of their plans, we were ignorant. It was resolved that I should go on another mission towards what was called " upper Tories," to find out something, if practicable. I was mounted on a pretty fleet nag, with orders to proceed with great caution. I started on Saturday morning, took a circuitous route, and went on until I had proceeded more than twenty miles, when I got to the house of a man by the name of Oats, on whom I could rely. He had a young man living with him whom he had raised from a child, being an orphan, named Crago. This man lived near a strong Tory settlement, and was obliged to act with the greatest caution. Crago was quite a pleasant fellow, well acquainted among them, and appeared to be a great favorite with the old women and boys. He had often been among them, cock fighting, which was a favorite sport in those days, and he was thought to be a great hand at the business. It was agreed that Crago should ride with me next day, being Sunday. I was to pass as a companion of Crago's, and be altogether careless, while Crago, in his own way, should elicit all the news he could. It was understood, at the same time, that most of the men were from home, except the old ones, a sure sign that there was a movement on foot; but not having fully ascertained it, we started on our journey, halted at three or four houses, and found no one at home, but some women and boys. They all saluted Crago with some degree of kindness, yet we could get no satisfactory news. They would all inquire if there was any news from Moffitt, and make remarks intimating that he would meet with a check before long. At length we came to another house, got off our horses and went in; here Crago, as usual, began to chat with the old woman. It was my wish, and Crago knew it, that I did not want to be known by name. I had taken up an old book that lay close at hand, and was perusing the same, when an old man entered the house, who had been out somewhere. He saluted Crago, glanced his eye at me, and spoke to me. After talking to Crago a few moments, he turned around on his seat and said, "what young man is this you have with you?" "Oh, it's a young man that lives away down yonder by my uncle's." "Well," said the old man, "what news from your uncle's?—are all well?" "Oh, yes." "Well, does the young man bring any news from Moffitt and his gang and what they are doing?" "Oh, no, he is a young man that has been working at the tailor business down by uncle's and knows nothing about Moffitt, for they never go in that quarter; they are always about Broad River or Ticketty, or lower down." "Well," said the old man, "be they where they may, I think they will get something to do before long. There is a great meeting of our friends to take place upon Buffalo, next Thursday night, at Elliot's, and they are going to send down to the Brushy Fork and Sandy River boys to be ready to join them, and I think if they all get together they will soon settle the business with Moffitt and all his gang. There will be another meeting on the South Fork about

Ramsour's before long; so I think we will have the country clear before long." "Well," said Crago, "I wish they may have good luck for the times are troublesome; I wish they may settle it at once." "Settle it," exclaimed the old man, "if they would all give up as they ought to do, and as they will be compelled to do at last, they might easily settle it and save a great many lives and save their property besides; but it will be settled to their cost and that before long—you will see it then. The King has men enough to conquer them without help and more than half the people are on his side."

All this time I had confined myself closely to my book, not saying a word on either side, hoping my silence would keep me from being questioned—and it did. It will here be remembered, that I and Crago had often been together before, and were no strangers to each other. We took dinner with the old man and left him with the spirit of prophecy still hanging upon him. Crago and I returned to my friend Oats, in the evening, and communicated the outlines of our adventure, staying all night. In the morning early, I started on my way back, taking a different route from that which I had gone. After riding some ten or twelve miles, I had to fall into a main road that passes through the gap of King's mountain. At this place lived a man by the name of Dixon. a little advanced in years, having a family—daughters, five in number, and two small boys. He was in good circumstances for the times, and lived in a very public place, situated on the northern road, where all, passing from above or below, had to cross the mountain, and there was no other house on the road for about twenty miles. He kept a good farm and consequently was in a way of making something. Here I halted, my appetite being up, to get something to eat. I was well acquainted with this man and his family, and was under no apprehension of danger, seated at the table, with some bread, butter, and milk before me, which I was always fond of. While I was thus enjoying my meal, an old woman and a boy rode up to the gate, mounted on a couple of small nags, with some baggage on each. They alighted without ceremony, came in the house, and appeared quite familiar with the place. "Good morning, Mr. Dixon," said the woman. "Good morning, Mrs. Hedgepith," he replied, shaking hands very cordially. The old lady drew a pipe out of her pocket, went to the fire, after saluting all the females, filled her pipe, and lighting the same, commenced smoking. "La me! Mr. Dixon," said she, "I want something to eat for myself and little son; we have been riding all morning—have not had a mouthful to eat and feel hungry." "How far have you come?" said Mr. Dixon. "Why, clear from Mr. Hopes, away down yonder. I would have stopped at your brother's, but I was afraid; for they are a bad set down about your brother's there, you know. It was late too, but I was afraid, and I kept on all the way to Mr. Hope's, and it was some time in the night before I got there. Mr. Hope asked us to stay and get breakfast, but I was in a hurry and could not stay: I thought I would stop at Henry's, but there was five or six men there, and I did not like to stop, for that is another bad place you know. I was afraid they would serve me like they did the last time I was up there; I came up the other road, for it is the nighest; I met with some of Moffitt's set and they took away my little son's beast, and left us one between us. I had papers then, and do you think they didn't search all my pockets and took all my papers, and my little boy's beast in the bargain. But I brought no papers this time; so I think they will hardly find out my business this time." I happened to be present at the time of the search, and discovery of the papers, and immediately recognized the old woman and her son, and kept silent all the while she was talking. The lady of the house observed she had nothing cooked or ready, and told her she had better have her horses stripped and wait for dinner, which would not be long, saying at the same time, "Come girls, it is time you were getting dinner." "Oh, la! I cannot wait," said the old woman, "I am in a great hurry; I am obliged to be back day-after-to-morrow. A little bread and milk will do if you have it—I cannot wait for dinner." "Well," said the woman, "I have plenty of bread and milk, but I would rather you would stay and get something better." "Oh, la, no! no, I think I cannot stay." So the bread and milk being prepared, the woman and son commenced on it with a good grace. The man of the house winked at me, and began some inquiries. "Well," said he, "what is all the news below?" Oh, la, dear me! there is none very good about us; there is that old turkey-cock of a Sumpter just below us and he has a troublesome set about him—we can get no rest for them; and there's Moffitt and his set has been down close by us, not long since—I wonder where abouts he is now?—haven't heard lately." The old man said, "they *were* down about Turkey Creek; where they are now I know not." "Oh," said the old woman, "I believe it is hard to tell where they are, for they never stay long in one place; but they will all get plenty to do before long—they will find warmer times than when they killed Lord Hook. There's Neel, and Watson, and Moffitt, and even old Billy Hill must have had a hand in the business. I wish Billy Hill had another set of iron-works to burn down; I'll be bound he would soon have it done for him,—and there is old Brattin and Frank Ross are no better than the rest; they will get plenty to do before long to keep them from searching old women's pockets. The Sandy River Boys are fixing for them, and they have heard that the Upper Boys are getting ready to help them—I have come up to see when they will be ready, and hurry them on. The Sandy River Boys will all be ready by Saturday next, and they want the Upper Boys to meet them on Sunday. I am going up to old friend Ponder's; he has some sons, smart fellows; I know they will help, and then I will go up to Floyd's; there will be more help, and I know they will hurry on the others; when they all get together I think they will be able to settle with

Moffitt, if they find him, and they will soon hunt him up. I wonder your brother don't know better; he has some five sons and he will ruin them all." "Ah," said Dixon. "I have talked with him on the subject, but there is no doing anything with him: when he puts his head to anything he will have his own way; and in fact he had two sons with Moffitt at the time you allude to—the killing of Lord Hook."

One of the young women gave me a significant look, in which I thought there was some meaning, and walked out of the house. There was a loomhouse stood close in the yard; she entered it and commenced weaving. Such was my confidence in the family, that I thought they would conceal me by any means, if any possible danger should approach, and I have not changed my opinion yet, and have often thought that women were better calculated for an enterprise of that kind, and imminent emergencies, than men. I walked slowly, and passed through the yard, near the door of the loomhouse, which stood open. The young woman beckoned me to come in; I entered, when she observed to me, "You had better not stay here too long; there are three of those upper fellows now gone below —they passed here this morning, and have gone down to Clark's Fork, five or six miles below; I expect they are gone to try to get some others about that part of the country to join them in their meeting alluded to by that old woman in the house; they said they were going to old G——s, and there is quite a number who will be sure to help them." "You had better," continued she, "leave the road here, and go down by the way of McArthur's: it is very little out of the way, and then you will fall into the road near Henry's, where you will be safe. If you should keep the road you are now on, and should meet any of those lower fellows, you will be known and your situation will be unpleasant; it is too perilous a task for you to undertake. I entreat you take my advice this time; the old woman will not find out anything about you." In a few minutes I was mounted on my horse and was off in a tangent. I took the way the young lady advised me, and passed on without interruption. In the meantime, Moffitt had moved off from the place where I left him stationed, about four miles, in order to be near a blacksmith shop, but care was taken that I should be directed to the place. Late in the evening I arrived at the place of my destination. I found all the men busy. I gave as correct an account as I could of all I had seen or heard during my absence, which was listened to with earnestness by all who heard me.

It will be, perhaps, proper here to mention, that we were a set of men acting entirely on our own footing, without the promise or expectation of any pay. There was nothing furnished us from the public; we furnished our own clothes, composed of coarse materials. and all home spun; our over dress was a hunting shirt, of what was called linsey woolsey, well belted around us. We furnished our own horses, saddles, bridles, guns, swords, butcher knives, and our own spurs; we got our powder and lead as we could, and had often to apply to the old women of the country, for their old pewter dishes and spoons, to supply the place of lead; and if we had lead sufficient to make balls, half lead and the other pewter, we felt well supplied. Swords, at first, were scarce, but we had several good blacksmiths among us; besides, there were several in the country. If we got hold of a piece of good steel, we would keep it; and likewise, go to all the sawmills, and take all the old whip saws we could find, set three or four smiths to work, in one shop, and take the steel we had, to another. In this way, we soon had a pretty good supply of swords and butcher knives. Mostly all of our spurs, bridle bits, and horsemen's caps, were manufactured by us. We would go to a turner or wheelwright, and get head blocks turned, of various sizes, according to the heads that had to wear them, in shape resembling a sugar loaf; we would then get some strong upper, or light sole leather, cut it out in shape, close it on the block, then grease it well with tallow, and set it before a warm fire, still on the block, and keep turning it round before the fire, still rubbing on the tallow, until it became almost as hard as a sheet of iron ; we then got two small straps or plates of steel, made by our own smiths, of a good spring temper, and crossing in the centre above, one reaching from ear to ear, the other, in the contrary direction ; the lining was made of strong cloth, padded with wool, and fixed so as to prevent the cap from pressing too hard on the ears ; there was a small brim attached to the front, resembling the caps now worn, a piece of bear skin lined with strong cloth, padded with wool, passed over from the front to the back of the head ; then a large bunch of hair taken from the tail of a horse, generally white, was attached to the back part and hung down the back ; then, a bunch of white feathers, or deer's tail, was attached to the sides, which completed the cap. The cap was heavy, but custom soon made it so that it could be worn without inconvenience. We made the scabbards of our swords of leather, by closing on a pattern of wood, and treating it similar to the cap. Our swords and knives, we polished mostly with a grindstone—not a very fine polish to be sure ; but they were of a good temper, sharpened to a keen edge, and seldom failed to do execution, when brought into requisition.

At these occupations they were busily engaged, when I returned from my last excursion. My communication had been received in private, only by the Colonel and a few of his confidential officers, and I was peremptorily charged not to divulge the communication to any one. In fact when I was sent out on any similar occasion, the business was known only to the colonel and my father, and by the way, my father was promoted to the rank of a brigade major. The troops still continued their preparations for battle until Wednesday evening, when we were all paraded, and orders given to every man to look to his gun, and see that it was in good order, report the amount of his stock of powder and balls, see that it was in good order, and be ready to march at a minute's warning, on the next morning. Most of the troops had by this time been pretty well furnished with swords; for my own part I received one, the first I had ever used. We carried no camp equipage, no cooking utensils, nor any thing to encumber us; we depended on what chance or kind providence might cast in our way, and were always ready to decamp in a short time, so that we were what might be called the harum-scarum-ramstan boys—the ranting squad. Next morning pretty early, we were mounted and under marching orders; few could guess the object, but it was evident that there was something in the wind; we steered on in nearly a northern direction, so that if our movement should be noticed, it might seem that we were rather marching for Ramsour's, the other contemplated place of rendezvous. In the evening, we turned more to the west until we were within about twelve miles of the intended place; here we halted near a farm, where we knew we had friends, and obtained some provisions, and forage for our horses. After placing out guards, we were directed to keep our horses with the saddles, lie down on our arms, and be ready when called. We all laid down, the weather was warm and we needed no fires; some perhaps did not sleep, but for my part, I fell asleep immediately: however, not many hours had passed until we were called up, without much noise, and the nature of the movement explained to all. We then mounted our horses, when profound silence was enjoined on all. We had good guides, who took the lead, and all followed; not long before day, we crossed the creek at a short distance above the place of our destination; we halted and sent out spies on foot, to ascertain the position of the enemy, who soon returned bringing intelligence that the enemy were posted in a large log building, having three guards placed out—one in the yard and the other two at no great distance from each end of a long lane, through which the main road passed by the house.

As soon as day broke, we again moved on slowly, and in

silence, keeping the strip of woods between us and the building, in order to gain the main road, if possible, undiscovered. We succeeded—got close to the road, halted, and again sent out two or three men to make what discovery they could. They soon returned, reporting that the house doors were open, that the enemy were passing in and out, and appeared to apprehend no alarm. We then formed into regular order, the sun now being up, moved on, and were within a short distance of the guard before we were discovered. The enemy began to rally, but they had no time—we were too close upon them ; they fired a few guns, but without effect, and fled, some leaving their guns ; we were in the yard by the time they issued from the house. As we entered the yard. their leader came out, storming at his men. He was shot down, and two others fell by his side, with several of the guard ; the other guard advanced, but the rifle balls stopped their progress, and they soon retreated. In an instant, after entering the yard, some of our men rushed into the house ; the windows flew open, and the enemy tumbled out, one over the other. Numbers of them fell in their hurry, and ran some distance on all fours before they could recover their legs. Others went helter skelter, most of them bareheaded, for a large swamp on the creek, not far distant, though several were compelled to halt by the way from the effect of our rifle balls. We took possession of most of their guns, which were stacked in the yard, and also took several of them prisoners ; likewise, most of their ammunition, swords, and pistols. When all was over, we found that we had killed three of their best officers, and five others ; sixteen were badly wounded.

On a large table set some decanters or rather cased bottles, with some peach brandy in them ; our colonel ordered the man of the house who had surrendered on our first entering, to produce some more of his brandy, which was done. The men were all paraded and the roll called ; it was found that all were present, and not a man hurt. We all all fell in ranks and foaming with sweat, and thirsty from the effect of the powder, every man received one glass of brandy and no more. We next began to look out for something for our horses, and something for ourselves to eat, with both of which we were bountifully supplied. We then selected a few of the enemy's best rifles and whatever of the swords were deemed sufficient to stand service—breaking the others. We then took all the pistols we could find, and holsters, such as we thought would answer our purpose, breaking the locks of the others and throwing them away, as unfit for further use. We took care of the powder and balls, and the guns we used similar to the pistols—breaking the locks and mainsprings. Here I had fired my little blue barrel twice, for I still carried her, but I suspect without effect as usual, for the second time I fired, it was at a man who tumbled out of a window at a short distance; I thought that I would stop his progress, but he scampered off without halting. Here I came in possession of a brace of excellent pistols, and the most of our men that lacked swords were furnished. We exchanged two or three of our horses, that were almost tired down for the same number of the best that they had. All things now being arranged, we mounted and formed in order, when each man received a small glass of the peach again, and moving off, left the dead to bury their dead.

CHAPTER IV.

SKIRMISH WITH THE ENEMY.

DIRECTING our course down Broad River, we then marched, after thus defeating the designs and stratagems of old Jezebel, which she had concerted—to put Naboth to death and obtain the vineyard. Her schemes were all baffled, and so it would appear from the whole history of this manoeuvre; we, resting our hopes under the strong and protecting arm of freedom, which has paved the way and laid the foundation of this great Republic. She had this time carried no papers to betray her. We moved on some miles, and encamped for the night, using at the same time every precaution, knowing that we were among enemies. Next morning, we learned that there was a party gathering below us, at one Harrison's, a noted Tory. We immediately marched for the place, but when we arrived there, all was silent, and not a man to be seen. One of those Ponders, of whom I have spoken, being an active man, had turned out in order to raise some recruits, for the purpose of strengthening the parties contemplated by the old Jezebel. They had collected, but by some means had got wind of us. When we arrived, there were several women about the house; inquiry was made if there had been some men there that morning? The reply was in the affirmative but they had gone two hours or more. "Which way did they go?" "Oh! they went off down that way some place, but we don't know where." We moved off our road, passed round part of the farm, and a rough thicket on the other side. Before we had proceeded far one of our men observed: "I don't like the looks of those women; those fellows are not far off, perhaps looking at us now." We had not proceeded more than half way round the fence, when all at once we were saluted with the report of twenty or perhaps thirty guns out of the thicket, and the whizzing of the balls about our heads. Down came two of our men just ahead of where I was; one soon recovered his feet, but the other in attempting to rise would stagger and fall. The thicket was not very extensive and a part of the men in front dashed on to go round it: some in the rear wheeled the other way, while a number of the centre dismounted near the wounded to defend them. In a few moments four men advanced from the thicket, within a short distance, Ponder being at their head. I saw my father level his gun at Ponder; both fired nearly at the same instant; Ponder's gun fell from his hands; Ponder wheeled and moved off in haste, leaving his gun, the others following his example. A few guns fired on the other side of the thicket; the enemy had retreated down a steep hill into a creek swamp, pursued by our men, who soon returned. It was discovered that one of the men who fell at the first fire, by the name of Watson, a lieutenant, was uninjured; his horse was shot dead under him. The other, named Burns, was shot in the hip, the ball passing through the hind tree of his saddle, entered his hip and lodged against the bone, just below the hip-joint. We picked up Ponder's gun, an excellent rifle, then supporting our wounded man on a horse, we bore him to a house at no great distance, where we constructed a litter and conveyed him to a place of safety. The ball was extracted, and it was but a few weeks until he was again in the field. In a few days we ascertained that Ponder had been shot through the wrist, so as to prevent him from using a gun any more. Harrison was slightly wounded through the fleshy part of the arm. In a few days it was ascertained that the meeting had taken place at Ramsour's. We mustered and started for the place, but we were too late; we arrived at the place in the evening, where we found our friends instead of enemies. A Capt. Falls, with some other officers, and a party of men from North Carolina, had attacked them in the early part of the day, and entirely defeated them; there were several killed on both sides and among the rest Capt. Falls himself lay dead. After assisting some of the wounded and helping to bury the dead belonging to our own side, we retreated to our own place. The Tory party on the west side of Broad River, were numerous; they began to muster up and threaten us; they commenced house burning and plundering. Among their leaders was one called Bill Cunningham, a man that will be execrated by some of the descendants of the sufferers, perhaps to generations yet unborn. Women were insulted, and stripped of every particle of decent clothing they might have on, and every article of bedding, clothing or furniture was taken—knives, forks, dishes, spoons, in fact everything that could be carried off. Not a piece of meat or a pint of salt was left. They even entered houses where men lay sick of the small-pox, that they knew were opposed to them, dragged them out of their sick beds into the yard and put them to death, in cold blood, in presence of their wives and children, or relatives. We were too weak to repel them, and it seemed as though they had been let loose from the bottomless pit, to execute infernal vengeance on all that disobeyed the mandates of the British. It seemed like our time, to suffer in the flesh, was at hand. In order to save ourselves a little longer, it was determined to join Sumpter, below, but we jumped out of the frying pan into the fire; we met Sumpter retreating rapidly; we joined in the retreat until we came to Fishing Creek. a place where it was thought we could halt in safety, and rest, but not so. Sumpter encamped on the main road, near the creek ; we were encamped a short distance above, on his left, where another road crossed the creek ; there was a guard or picket posted at a short distance in the rear ; the men were all fatigued ; some had kindled fires and were cooking and eating ; others tumbled down and were fast asleep, and all scattered in every direction. We had drawn some provisions, and forage for our horses, and were engaged in about the same way, with, however, but few asleep. Our horses were mostly close at hand, and but few saddles off ; all at once the picket guns gave the alarm—they retreated on the main body with the enemy at their heels. Before Sumpter could wake up his men and form, the enemy were among them cutting down everything in their way. Sumpter, with all the men he had collected, retreated across the creek at the main road, leaving the remainder to the mercy of the enemy. It was a perfect rout, and an indiscriminate slaughter. No quarter was given ; we were preparing in all haste to secure our own safety. The greater part of our number dashed through the creek, at the fording place, and pushing on with all possible speed, reached the highland. After we had gotten fairly to the top of the hill, we halted. No enemy appeared, and we remained quiet for some time, waiting for some of our men, who were missing ; but no tidings—no one, neither friend or foe appearing. There had been but little firing, except the pistols of the enemy, and all seemed to be silent. At length a few blasts of the bugle brought some of our men in sight, who in their hurry had missed the fording place, and had gone up the creek where they found it difficult to pass, and were looking for our trail. Near sunset, a few more came up, but there were still some missing, of whom we could hear nothing. We then left the road, keeping a high, open ridge and went off some distance ; night coming on, we dismounted in the woods and tied our horses ; we had nothing for man or beast to eat, and the weather being warm, (August,) we kindled no fires. We lay down, every man with his sword by his side, his gun in his hands, and his pistol near his head. All were silent, for we expected the whole army had been taken prisoners, or put to the sword.

After I had laid down, I began to reflect. Well, thought I, if this be the fate of war, I would willingly be excused. I devised several plans to get out of the scrape, but none appeared likely to have the desired effect. The thing had gone too far, and there was no safety in retreating. At length, weary with thinking, I fell asleep. Before it was light, in the morning, we were all up, and on enquiry, it was found that five of our number were missing. It was resolved that we should return to the battle ground; a few spies having been sent forward, we follo ed at some distance. When we arrived, there was no appearance of the enemy—all was silent. In a few moments, a party of Sumpter's men made their appearance, crossing the creek. The dead and wounded lay scattered in every direction over the field; numbers lay stretched cold and lifeless; some were yet struggling in the agonies of death, while here and there, lay others, faint with the loss of blood, almost famished for water, and begging for assistance. The scene before me, I could not reconcile to my feelings, and I again began to repent that I had ever taken any part in the matter; however, by custom, such things become familiar. We commenced our search, and soon found two of our own party, one named Enloe, and the other Jackson, some distance apart, both setting up, unable to walk without assistance, and mangled by the sword. The other three we could not find among the living or the dead; what their fate was, we never knew, for we never heard of them afterwards. One was a lieutenant named Bryan, one of our most active men. We collected all the wounded we could; but poor fellows, we had little nourishment to give them; they all craved water, and even the little they received, seemed to revive them. We then began to look out some provisions, for ourselves and horses; we found corn lying about in many places, that had not been consumed the day before, and there were several kettles setting about, where the fire had been kindled, with provisions ready cooked—and provisions scattered about on the ground in various places. There was no time for choosing, and every man ate whatever he got hold of, asking no questions; then, taking a glass of cold water, we all felt somewhat braced up. There were several horses grazing about the old field, that appeared to be nearly worn out, some with bridles and saddles on, others without.

The guns lay scattered over the field, also various articles of camp equipage. Among the guns there was one picked up, a good looking rifle, with a shot-bag and all the apparatus belonging. The gun had apparently been laid down by some one who intended taking a little sleep, in order to have her ready when he awoke. The gun was presented to the Colonel, and after viewing her some time, he observed " Well, boys I have a use for this gun—I shall have to claim her as my part of the spoils." Then calling me up, said, "Well, James, you have been wanting a rifle for some time; here is one I think will suit you; she is light, and I think, a good one; she has an excellent lock; lay down your little shot-gun; take her, and take good care of her; I think you can do better with her than with the little shot-gun." A Capt. Chambers, who stood by, exclaimed, "That is right colonel, you have made a good disposition of the gun. I hope we shall have need of James, yet; he seems to be a lucky boy, and it is well to encourage him." I confess it had the effect of a stimulent, and in some measure reconciled me to my lot. After giving what help we could in burying the dead, in haste,—poor fellows it was badly done,—we caught two of the best looking horses we could find, and placing our two wounded men upon them, and supporting them as well as we could, we moved off, taking with us no plunder, (or very little) of what was considered of right to belong to Sumpter's men, being the property of their companions who had fallen. All the baggage, and everything valuable, had fallen into the hands of the enemy, and they had taken it off. We got to a house, a few miles distant, where we obtained some nourishment for the wounded, and finding an old horse-cart, we placed them in it, and next day, got them to their home, where they both recovered, but not without being much disfigured by their wounds.

CHAPTER V.

SCOUTING.

IN A BAD BOX, we now were, for the enemy was increasing in power. There was a small section of country that was united, lying partly in North, and partly in South Carolina. To this we were confined; we kept a flying camp, never staying long in one place—never camping near a public road. We were often invited by our friends, who were able to afford it, to partake of a dinner prepared for us; in these cases there was a long table, prepared of planks, set in an open place, at some distance from the house. Never stripping off saddles, and only unbitting our bridles, our horses were put to feed, placing a guard over them, and then placing out sentinels; each one sat down with his sword by his side; his gun lying across his lap, or under the seat on which he sat, and so eating in his turn, until all were done, and then often as playful as though there was no danger; we then mounted our horses and moved off. We were sometimes divided into two companies, still keeping up a communication, so as to know the movements of each other. While lying at camp, one day, on the background of a large farm of one of our friends, the report came in that a large party of Tories were advancing to invade our territory, and give us a scourging, and get some plunder. After some consultation among the officers, the colonel called me up, saying: "James, I have some business for you to do, and recollect, much depends on your performance." Then giving the outlines of the duty required, said, "You are acquainted with all the passways—you are light and a good rider; I will send James Kidd with you." He was a little more talkative than myself, but by no means inferior as a rider. "You must by all means avoid being taken prisoner, for much depends on your safe return."

There was a place about five or six miles distant where two public ways met; a large farm extended all around the buildings; there were three lanes by this place through which the enemy must necessarily pass, to arrive at the place where we encamped. We were directed to go and gain information; the owner of the farm was with us in camp, and was afraid to appear at home. In the evening, about sunset, we approached the end of one of the lanes, and taking a view, could see no kind of danger: we then rode up to the house, concluding if danger appeared in one lane, we could run out at the other. The woman of the house informed us, that she had had intelligence in the early part of the day, that the enemy were not far distant, and were momentarily expected; that they could not be, according to the best information, more than two miles distant. By this time, it was in the dusk of the evening. Seeing no danger, we rode off through one of the lanes, and after passing out a little distance on the way that we intended taking, turned off; just as we arrived at the spot, we heard some noise ahead—we halted and discovered a crowd advancing—we wheeled off in silence, but were discovered—they hailed us but we made no reply, hoping they would not pursue. In a moment a voice roared out, "Stop, you d——d rascals, or we will shoot you." There was was a small creek ahead—we passed that at a pretty brisk rate, when we heard the pursuit commence, and a voice exclaim, "Damn the buggers, we will have them!" "In a minute, now," thought I; "do thy speedy utmost, 'Meg,' or I may be troubled with a halter." I reckon that Tam O'Shanter did not urge his flight with more energy from the witches of Kirk Alloway, than we did. We were well mounted and unincumbered, which perhaps gave us some advantage. Having confidence in my nag and my own horsemanship, and knowing my companion to be nothing inferior, we pressed on at full speed. After running about a mile, or perhaps a little more, we completely distanced our pursuers. There was a small path turned off to the right, which we intended taking; we suddenly tacked, and after leaving the road a short distance, we halted and stood still. The noise of their own horses had prevented them from hearing our tack—they came on under a crowd of sail, and went along the road—we could see their shadows as they passed, but it was too dark to count them. After they had passed us we moved off a short distance farther and remained silent; after some time, they returned along the road, talking pretty loud, and making some remarks about the chase. As soon as they were out of hearing, we moved off in silence, and in a short time arrived at camp to make our report.

How many were in pursuit of us, I know not—it would seem to me, from the noise there must have been ten or a dozen. It was determined that next morning we should fall on their rear, and give them a brush, but we were too late—they had taken a different direction from the one calculated, and before we could strike their trail they were too far gone for us to pursue them in safety.

CHAPTER VI.

BATTLE OF KING'S MOUNTAIN.

AT THIS TIME, there was Clarke, from Georgia, with his adherents, driven to take refuge in the confines of North Carolina. There was a communication between him and Moffitt. There were two parties of Tories posted on the west side of Broad River; one at a place called Black Stock. the other, lower down at a place called Musgrove's Mills. It was agreed that we should attack both places at the same time, if possible. It fell to our lot to attack at Black Stock, while Clarke was to attack Musgrove's; both parties succeeded in driving away the enemy. We had five men wounded—three badly though not mortally, the other two slightly; while Clarke had several wounded and one or two killed. What number the enemy lost I cannot say at this time, but they had several killed and wounded at both places. We all took care to secure what powder and balls we could in such cases, never encumbering ourselves with heavy plunder. As soon as the business was over, we fixed up our wounded as well as we could, and moved off. We had not proceeded far, till we fell in with a number of families, perhaps fifty, or more, pushing on with all possible speed to take refuge in North Carolina. Some had wagons, some had packs, all the company being, old men, women, and boys. We placed our wounded in some of the wagons, and guarded the whole until we got across Broad River; we then took the wounded and conveyed them to a place of safety, where they recovered. Among the wounded, was one of our best blacksmiths, by the name of Shaw. In a few weeks our danger began to increase; Ferguson was coming on with his boasted marksmen, and seemed to threaten the destruction of the whole country. The Tories were flocking to his standard from every quarter, and there appeared little safety for us; but as God would have it, a patriotic party sprung up about Hillsboro, North Carolina, under Colonels Campbell, Williams, Shelby, and Cleveland; Sevier, from the mountains, joined in, together with Hamright, and some other leaders. As they advanced their numbers kept augmenting: our chance of safety was to join, if possible, the advancing patriots, to accomplish which, we passed on through North Carolina; but before we reached them, the army had passed. We fell in their rear, took their trail, and pushed on till we overtook them without being intercepted. It had been expected, that Ferguson would cross Broad River, high up, and they would meet him on his march. But he had turned his course; took a road to the right, and steered more to the east, towards Charlotte in North Carolina, thus steering right through our section of country. Our army fell in his rear, at no great distance behind and took his trail and commenced pursuit. The spies brought in news that he had crossed Broad River at a place called the Cherokee Ford, and had made a stand. He had taken a position at a small distance down the river, below the crossing place; having the river on one side, a high rocky ridge on the other, and a large old field fronting where we must of necessity cross the river. The pursuing army had not a single baggage waggon or any kind of camp equipage; every one ate what he could get, and slept in his own blanket, sometimes eating raw turnips, and often resorting to a little parched corn, which by the by, I have often thought, if a man would eat a mess of parched corn and swallow two or three spoonfuls of honey, then take a good draught of cold water, he could pass longer without suffering than with any other diet he could use. On Friday evening, we came to the river, with the the full expectation of meeting them, and being attacked in crossing: we passed over but no enemy appeared. The enemy had moved on, I think, about nine miles, and made a stand on a place called King's Mountain, and determined to give battle. We had encamped for the night, on the ground the enemy had left; on Saturday morning, October 7th, 1780, we were paraded, and harangued in a short manner, on the prospect before us. The sky was overcast with clouds, and at times a light mist of rain falling; our provisions were scanty, and hungry men are apt to be fractious; each one felt his situation; the last stake was up and the severity of the game must be played; everything was at stake—life, liberty, property, and even the fate of wife, children and friends, seemed to depend on the issue; death or victory was the only way to escape suffering. Near two o'clock in the afternoon we came in sight of the enemy, who seemed to be fully prepared to give battle at all risks. When we came up, we halted, and formed in order of battle. Shelby happened to be in command that day as every colonel took command day about. The men were disposed of in three divisions—the right was commanded by Cleveland and Sevier, the left by Campbell and Williams, and the centre by Shelby and Hamright. The enemy was posted on a high, steep and rugged ridge, or spur of the mountain, very difficult of access, with a small stream of water running on each side: along each stream was a narrow strip of flat ground. The plan was, to surround the mountain and attack them on all sides, if possible. In order to do this, the left had to march under the fire of the enemy to gain the position assigned to them, on the stream on the right of the enemy, while the right was to take possession of the other stream; in doing this they were not exposed, the cliff being so steep as to cover them completely. Each leader made a short speech in his own way to his men, desiring every coward to be off immediately; here I confess I would willingly have been excused, for my feelings were not the most pleasant—this may be attributed to my youth, not being quite seventeen years of age—but I could not well swallow the appellation of coward. I looked around; every man's countenance seemed to change; well, thought I, fate is fate, every man's fate is before him and he has to run it out, which I am inclined to think yet. I was commanded this day by Major Chronicle and Capt. Watson. We were soon in motion, every man throwing four or five balls in his mouth to prevent thirst, also to be in readiness to reload quick. The shot of the enemy soon began to pass over us like hail; the first shock was quickly over, and for my own part, I was soon in a profuse sweat. My lot happened to be in the centre, where the severest part of the battle was fought. We soon attempted to climb the hill, but were fiercely charged upon and forced to fall back to our first position; we tried a second time, but met the same fate; the fight then seemed to become more furious. Their leader, Ferguson, came in full view, within rifle shot as if to encourage his men, who by this time were falling very fast; he soon disappeared. We took to the hill a third time; the enemy gave way; when we had gotten near the top, some of our leaders roared out, "Hurra, my brave fellows! Advance! They are crying for quarter"

By this time, the right and left had gained the top of the cliff; the enemy was completely hemmed in on all sides, and no chance of escaping—besides, their leader had fallen. They soon threw down their arms and surrendered. After the fight was over, the situation of the poor Tories appeared to be really pitiable; the dead lay in heaps on all sides, while the groans of the wounded were heard in every direction. I could not help turning away from the scene before me, with horror, and though

exulting in victory, could not refrain from shedding tears.—
"Great God!" said I, "Is this the fate of mortals, or was it for this cause that man was brought into the world?"

On examining the dead body of their great chief, it appeared that almost fifty rifles must have been leveled at him, at the same time; seven rifle balls had passed through his body, both of his arms were broken, and his hat and clothing were literally shot to pieces. Their great elevation above us had proved their ruin; they overshot us altogether, scarce touching a man, except those on horseback, while every rifle from below, seemed to have the desired effect. In this conflict I had fired my rifle six times, while others had perhaps fired nine or ten. I had by this time learned to shoot a rifle pretty well, was not a bad hand in the second class, and had come to this conclusion: never to retreat alone, shoot without an object, or lay down my gun until the last extremity; for, thought I, a gun, though empty, might keep an enemy at bay. Whether I effected any thing or not, is unknown to me. My first shot I ever doubted, for I really had a shake on me at the time; but that soon passed over, and I took the precaution to conceal myself as well as I could, behind a tree or rock, of which there were plenty, and take as good aim as possible.

Next morning, which was Sunday, the scene became really distressing; the wives and children of the poor Tories came in, in great numbers. Their husbands, fathers, and brothers, lay dead in heaps, while others lay wounded or dying; a melancholy sight indeed! while numbers of the survivors were doomed to abide the sentence of a court martial, and several were actually hanged. As regards the numbers that fell, authors have disagreed; yet none have overrated the number. I know our estimate, at the time, was something over three hundred.— We proceeded to bury the dead, but it was badly done; they were thrown into convenient piles, and covered with old logs, the bark of old trees, and rocks; yet not so as to secure them from becoming a prey to the beasts of the forest, or the vultures of the air; and the wolves became so plenty, that it was dangerous for any one to be out at night, for several miles around; also, the hogs in the neighborhood, gathered in to the place, to devour the flesh of men, inasmuch as numbers chose to live on litlle meat rather than eat their hogs, though they were fat; half of the dogs in the country were said to be mad, and were put to death. I saw, myself, in passing the place, a few weeks after, all parts of the human frame, lying scattered in every direction. As God would have it, there had but few of our men been slain—fifteen or sixteen—but of that number some of our bravest men; Colonels Williams and Hamright, with Majors Chronicle, and some other distinguished men, had fallen. These we buried in the flat ground under the hill, near where the battle commenced, and I expect their graves are to be seen there to this day.

Of the troop, or company, to which I belonged, we had two badly wounded; one, a lieutenant, by the name of Watson, the other, a private, named Caldwell; we carried them to their own homes, in the evening, where they both died, in a few days. Poor fellows! they were raised together, fought together, died nearly at the same time in the same house, and lie buried together. In the evening, there was a distribution made of the plunder, and we were dismissed. My father and myself drew two fine horses, two guns, and some articles of clothing, with a share of powder and lead; every man repaired to his tent, or home. It seemed like a calm, after a heavy storm had passed over, and for a short time, every man could visit his home, or his neighbor, without being afraid. After the result of the battle was known, we seemed to gather strength, for many that before lay neutral, through fear or some other cause, shouldered their guns, and fell in the ranks; some of them making good soldiers.

CHAPTER VII.

BATTLE OF THE COWPENS.

HOWEVER, affairs could not long remain in this situation. The British and Tories were still in strength below, and also on the west side of Broad River; besides, Georgia was infested with them. It became necessary for us to be again in motion; the Tories were mustering up in small parties, to seek revenge, and we again set out to chastise them. Those Ponders, of whom I have before spoken, were still using all their exertions. It was determined, if possible, to get hold of some of them. For that purpose, we passed above King's Mountain, and got into their ranging ground, but they eluded us. Here, I was put to a trial that I have not forgotten, nor never will forget. We had caught the old father of the clan that we were in search of; he was a very old, grayheaded man, and was brought before the colonel and threatened with instant death unless he would tell where his sons were. The old man declared he did not know, but being still threatened, he fell on his knees, laid off his hat and began to beg for his life. He no doubt thought his life was at stake. While he was in this situation a man in the company took me aside, and holding a long spear in his hand, with a handle perhaps six or eight feet long, said, "I want you to take this spear and run it through that d—d old

Tory; he ought to die." "No," said I, "he is too old; besides the colonel would never forgive me; he is a prisoner and he don't intend to kill him." "Oh," said he, "I can easily plead you off with the colonel;" then putting his hand in his pocket he drew out a purse of money, saying, "Here is twenty dollars—[showing the silver]—I will give you this to kill him." I felt insulted. I thought he underrated my real character, and thought that through my youth and inexperience, he would bribe me to do a deed that he himself would be ashamed of. I turned away, saying, "It will take but one to do it, and you can do it as easily as I can." I thank God, I escaped the temptation, for I verily believe had I committed the deed, the ghost of that old man would have haunted me to this day; but I thank God, I never had a desire to take away the life of any man, even my worst enemy. A man in battle, or in the heat of passion, might deem it necessary, but after much reflection, I am inclined to think that no man, possessed of the spirit of real patriotism, would seek revenge by taking away his enemy's life. At all events it gave me a dislike to the man that made the proposal, and I never thought favorably of him afterwards. I knew him a number of years after; he at last ran distracted and died so, and I have often thought that he was rotten at the core, and consequently remorse had overtaken him, for something wrong. However, the poor old Tory was set at liberty, after getting a friendly admonition from the colonel. It was not long until it became necessary for us to seek safety by joining Morgan, who was encamped at the Cowpens. but we were not permitted to remain long idle, for Tarleton came on like a thunder storm, which soon put us to our best mettle. After the tidings of his approach came into camp,—in the night,—we were all awakened, ordered under arms, and formed in order of battle by daybreak. About sunrise on the 17th January, 1781, the enemy came in full view. The sight, to me at least, seemed somewhat imposing; they halted for a short time, and then advanced rapidly, as if certain of victory. The militia under Pickins and Moffitt, was posted on the right of the regulars some distance in advance, while Washington's cavalry was stationed in the rear. We gave the enemy one fire, when they charged us with their bayonets; we gave way and retreated for our horses, Tarleton's cavalry pursued us; ("now," thought I, "my hide is in the loft;") just as we got to our horses, they overtook us and began to make a few hacks at some, however, without doing much injury. They, in their haste, had pretty much scattered, perhaps, thinking they would have another Fishing creek frolic, but in a few moments, Col. Washingion's cavalry was among them, like a whirlwind, and the poor fellows began to keel from their horses, without being able to remount. The shock was so sudden and violent, they could not stand it, and immediately betook themselves to flight; there was no time to rally, and they appeared to be as hard to stop as a drove of wild Choctaw steers, going to a Pennsylvania market. In a few moments the clashing of swords was out of hearing and quickly out of sight; by this time, both lines of the infantry were warmly engaged and we being relieved from the pursuit of the enemy began to rally and prepare to redeem our credit, when Morgan rode up in front, and waving his sword, cried out, "Form, form, my brave fellows! give them one more fire and the day is ours. Old Morgan was never beaten." We then advanced briskly, and gained the right flank of the enemy, and they being hard pressed in front, by Howard, and falling very fast, could not stand it long. They began to throw down their arms, and surrender themselves prisoners of war. The whole army, except Tarleton and his horsemen, fell into the hands of Morgan, together with all the baggage. After the fight was over, the sight was truly melancholy. The dead on the side of the British, exceeded the number killed at the battle of King's Mountain, being if I recollect aright, three hundred, or upwards. The loss, on the side of the Americans, was only fifteen or sixteen, and a few slightly wounded. This day, I fired my little rifle five times, whether with any effect or not, I do not know. Next day after receiving some small share of the plunder, and taking care to get as much powder as we could, we (the militia) were disbanded and returned to our old haunts, where we obtained a few day's rest.

CHAPTER VIII.

A HAZARDOUS ADVENTURE.

BUT OUR REST did not last long. About this time, Cornwallis commenced his pursuit of Morgan, and would consequently pass, with his whole army, within twelve miles of where we were. It was thought advisable, by Moffitt, to send some communication to Col. Davidson, who was encamped near Charlotte, in North Carolina. It was determined that I should become the bearer of the dispatches; the task was somewhat hazardous, for all parties were in motion, and times pretty squally. Col. Moffitt communicated the business to me alone, keeping it a profound secret from all the men, except three or four of his confidential officers; at the same time, secrecy was enjoined, advising great caution, and the avoidance of all public roads, as much as possible. In order to do this I was compelled to take a circuitous route. I was at that time acquainted with the country and all the private ways through which I had to pass. Laying aside all kinds of arms, and every thing that might make any show of hostility, putting on a hunting shirt and hat, and being lightly equipped, I was prepared to start. I was mounted on a mare that I commonly rode, not of the fleetest kind for a short distance, but of bottom sufficient to bear her out in a long race. The morning was far advanced when I started; I had perhaps gone four or five miles, when I was compelled to fall into a public road, which I had to keep for a short distance. When I entered the road, I looked to the right and saw a company of men, at a distance, coming at a smart gait. I thought from their appearance, they might be friends; but friends or foes, I had no wish to be examined; I therefore urged the pace of my nag a little. I looked back, and saw some of them beckoning for me to stop, but I did not obey the signal; I saw four of the company advance immediately to the front and put forward, in a brisk gallop, after me. I moved on, at about half speed, when my way turned off to the right; leaving the main road, I hoped the pursuit would end, but not so—it seemed rather to urge them on. They had by this time gained on me considerably, though not within shooting distance; they began to halloa to me to stop or they would fire. I then determined to try their speed; knowing that they were encumbered with their arms, and I thus having the advantage, I put my nag to the top of her speed and soon began to distance them. From where the race commenced, I had two miles to run to where there was a farm, and a long lane to pass through; I had a short hill to run down, and a small stream of water to cross, just before entering the lane. I gained the top of the hill in time to cross the stream before they came in sight. Just after crossing the stream, near the end of the lane, a small path turned off, that passed around the fence; I took the path before they came in view, and was soon out of sight, it being a pretty smart thicket where the path passed around the field. When they came in view of the lane I was missing, and they rode through the lane to a house, to make some inquiries; by this time I had reached the back part of the field, where I could have a fair view of the yard. Immediately, the whole company came up; the old man of the house was standing in the door, it being only a short distance from where I turned off, and told them the circumstance. He said he was confident that he knew me, and told them who I was. They were some of our own company, who had heard of a Tory party, that had started to make their way to Cornwallis, and they had started out to intercept them, if possible. When they heard who I was, the officer knew me, and concluded that I had fled through mistake, thinking it was the other party, and laughing heartily at his own men for being distanced. They turned back and took the road again; after they were fairly out of sight, I came back to the house, when the old man told me the whole story, and who they were. So I took my road, and went on without any further interruption.

It was impossible for me to reach the Catawba river before night, and the river being very wide and very rocky, and difficult to cross even in daylight, in the winter season, I thought it best not to attempt it in the night; therefore, I stopped, a short time after sunset, at the house of a man, named Turnbull, with whom I was acquainted, and told him I was going on a visit to a sister, living near Charlotte—the fact was, I had a sister there, and he knew it, so that saved me from any further explanation. I was on my way by daylight the next morning—I fell into the main road a short distance from the river, and crossed over in safety. I went on to Col. Davidson's camp, was hailed by the picket guard, and examined. I told the officer that I had communications to make to the commanding officer, to whom I was immediately conducted. I delivered my dispatches—he opened and read them; after asking me a few questions, he said: "Your Colonel confides very much in you, being so young." He then ordered my nag to be fed, and some refreshments prepared for myself. He kept his quarters in a house at the time, and invited me into a room where I got a glass of brandy, and some breakfast, for I had eaten nothing that day. After a short stay, myself and beast being refreshed, he gave me a paper to return to my own officer, advising me, at the same time, to use great caution, and ordered a guard to see me across the river. Accordingly, a sergeant, with four men, conducted me to the bank of the river, and there waited until I was safe on the other bank. I made no delay; after keeping the main road about half a mile, I turned off, taking a private way. I thought it best to vary my route a little, not returning exactly the same way I went. After leaving the main road about six miles, night came on, and I called at the house of a Mr. Spiers, a particular friend of my father. After alighting, I was shown into a room, where sat six well dressed men around a good fire, the weather being somewhat cold. After I was seated one of the company began to question me, and seemed to be more inquisitive than I wished him to be, while the others appeared to pay no attention, and sat conversing among themselves. I had no wish to explain anything, therefore I replied to his questions in as short a manner as possible, so as not to be abrupt, and affected to be ignorant, as I really was. I told him I had been over the river, on a visit to my sister's, and was returning home. "D——d ticklish times," said he, "for young men like you to be traveling about. Are you not afraid that Cornwallis or some of the Tories, will catch you and take you up?" "Not much;" said I, "they have no use for me." "Why," said he, "would you not fight?" "I should not like to fight," said I. "Ah, ha," said he, "they would soon learn you, and if you did not fight, by G—d, they would put you in a place to stop a bullet. Did you not see Davidson's men, when you were over the river?" "Yes." "Well, didn't they offer to take you up?" "No," said I, "they only served me like you do—asked me where I was going, and what I was after, and after that let me alone." I wished to get clear of his inquiries, if possible. I took him to be one of those waggish fellows, who wished to divert themselves and perhaps the company at the expense of others, without doing any great credit to their own wit. Mr. Spiers, who had been engaged out of doors, came in after dark, and asking me some questions, mentioned Moffitt's name, when my friend John, (for that was the only name by which I knew him,) said, "You live about Moffitt's, do you?"

"Yes, sir—in the neighborhood." "Well, where does he and his men keep themselves, now?" "I do not know;" was my answer, "the last I heard of them, they were over about Broad River." "Well, by G—d," said he, "if he don't look sharp his 'hide will be in the loft,' for Cornwallis is coming close by, and if he catches him, he'll show him no favors." "John," said Mr. Spiers "you are not perhaps well acquainted with Moffitt; he is not easily caught, and has men that will fight like tigers."

Here, I must mention a little anecdote. When supper came upon the table, there was a parcel of beef bones that appeared to have been well trimmed at dinner. There were two good-looking young ladies, whom I had frequently noticed passing about the house, and I thought from John's manner that he wished to attract their attention. They came to the table with an old lady that might have been their mother. The bone that fell to my lot, was a round joint with very little on it besides gristle, and my knife none of the sharpest; having eaten but once during the day, I was somewhat keen-set. After getting a few scanty mouthfuls, I made a rash cut to get a little deeper into the gristle, when my bone flew rapidly off my plate, and struck the partition wall, at a distance of some two or three feet, with considerable force. No one seemed to pay any attention; but my friend John, to add to my mortification, roared out "There, by G—d!—that has fled from its enemy." Mr. Spiers arose and placing another bone on my plate, something better than the first, said, "Don't mind him, young man, he is always running on with some foolishness." Then turning to John, said, "I wonder you can't let strangers alone." "By G—d," said John, "the fellow looks like he might want to go a courting, before long, and two or three such blunders might ruin his fortunes, forever." This sarcasm was by no means pleasant to my feelings, but I was obliged to stand it, and kept silent; the remainder of the company seemed to be collected in expectation of hearing some important news. After supper,

I got a bed as soon as possible, in order to avoid John's company. Before it was light, in the morning, all were up and stirring. I had my beast saddled, and ready to start by daylight; Mr. Spiers walked out with me to the gate, and was giving me some directions, when John came out into the yard, and cried out, "Mr. Spiers, that fellow is going off without paying his bill!" "No," said he, "all things are right;" at the same time requesting me not to answer John. As I rode off, John called out to me, "The Tories will catch you before night." I told him I thought not, and was soon out of sight. I had about thirty miles to ride, which I did without halting, and by noon, was among my companions, and delivered up my charge.

CHAPTER IX.

FERRETING OUT THE TORIES.

HE VERY NEXT NIGHT, Morgan, with his prisoners, lay at the same ford, where I had crossed the river—and Cornwallis was only one day's march behind him. There was much excitement through the whole country—scarce a man staid at home. Those that were not collected in parties, lay out in the woods; every article of furniture, clothing, or provisions—that was worth anything, was hid out; some in hollow trees, and often, hardware, that would stand it, was buried in the ground. A horse, that was worth any thing, was not to be seen, unless tied in some thicket, or perhaps, on some high open hill—where no one would go to look for property—and if a woman had but one quart of salt, to salt mush for her children, or a spoon to sup it with, she must keep it hid; or, if she had any decent apparel, she would scarce dare to wear it. Scouting parties, of both sides, were scouring the country in every direction.

But things did not **remain** long in this situation, for Cornwallis was marching rapidly on to Guilford, in North Carolina, when Gen. Green, meeting him and the Tories, gave him a smart check and they began to cool off a little in the parts where we were lying, high up in the country, about the 15th of March, 1781; but they still continued their depredations below. We were for the most part kept in motion, and considerably harassed until after the evacuation of Charleston by the British. Shortly after this event we commenced ferreting out the Tories, particularly the worst ones, and such as had been in the habit of plundering, burning and murdering. Those we called the "pet Tories," or neutrals, we never disturbed, but those that had been very troublesome, had to pay the piper. We would meet at a time and place appointed, probably at a church, schoolhouse, or some vacant building, generally in the afternoon, lay off our circuit and divide into two or more companies, and set off after dark. Wherever we found any Tories, we would surround the house, one party would force the doors and enter sword in hand, extinguish all the lights, if there were any, and suffer no light to be made, when we would commence hacking the man or men that were found in the house, threatening them with instant death, and occasionally making a furious stroke as if to dispatch them at once, but taking care to strike the wall or some object that was in the way, they generally being found crouched up in some corner, or about the beds. Another party would mount the roof of the house and commence pulling it down; thus the dwelling house, smoke house and kitchen, if any, were dismantled and torn down, at least to the joists. The poor fellows, perhaps expecting instant death, would beg hard for life, and make any promise on condition of being spared, while their wives or friends would join in their entreaties; on the condition that they would leave the country, within a specified time, and never return, they would suffer him to live, and I never knew an instance of one that failed to comply and numbers put off without any such measures being enforced. There was no property molested except the buildings, nor was there anything taken away. They were at liberty to do the best they could with everything but their lands; those they had to leave. These, I believe, escheated to the State, but I am not certain. There were none of the poor fellows much hurt, only they were hacked about their heads and arms enough to bleed freely. Many of the worst went among the different tribes of Indians, some went down the Mississippi River, about Natchez, and some to the Spanish country, Low Louisiana, others went to the frontiers of Georgia, and numbers to Tennessee and Kentucky; most of those who staid among civilized people became good citizens, good neighbors and men of respectability, many becoming very popular. I have seen many of them, years afterwards, that I knew well, but they did not recognize me, and I never mentioned it to any one. In those last mentioned excursions, I usually stood as the horse guard, or was posted in the yard, as sentinel, while the others were engaged in pulling down the house.

CHAPTER X.

RETURN HOME,

THE WAR being nearly settled, I returned home —but did not stay long. My father was a poor man, and had made nothing by the war; but, on the contrary, had lost a considerable share of what he had before; besides, his own time, and mine, on the farm, for nearly three years; he had also, a large family of children to support, and a probability of the number increasing. I was growing up— and my father, knowing that I had not the best feelings for my step-mother; although a fine woman, in many respects, I have thought and still think, that she did not treat me with that motherly affection and kindness, which she ought to have done. But she had a number of children of her own, and I suppose she thought it right to extend her partialities to them. There being no great prospect of making anything for myself, by remaining with my father, he advised me to turn out into the world, and do the best I could, at the same time, giving me good advice, as to the course I should pursue. Georgia was then a new country, and there was a chance of obtaining lands on good terms; my father advised me to make preparations and go there, and endeavor to secure some lands. My first object was money, which was very scarce and the wages for labor, low.

Before I could go to a new country, I must have some money, and I had no way to get it without labor. My father gave me a young horse, or rather a colt: I had a snug little rifle gun. I took my colt and gun, and went to a man, a great favorite of my father's, who was called a punctual and honest man, and a man of great industry, who wished to hire me. I had very little knowledge of mankind as to dealing and thought every man was what he pretended to be. We agreed that I should work for him a month, which was as long as he thought he would want me. He and I labored hard, together, late and early; we would sing a few psalms together, after supper every night, and after breakfast in the morning, which suited me very well for I had been accustomed to both. When my month expired, and we come to a sattlement, I found my colt was an expense for nothing, for I had to pay for his feed, and had no use for a horse—not even time to ride him. My friend McInnare, for that was his name, took or pretended to take a great fancy for my colt, and proposed to buy him. After beating me down in my price pretty smartly, he persuaded me that I ought never to allow my conscience to ask or take too much for anything, which doctrine I swallowed down, having often heard it preached before, and by that means he got my colt considerably under his real value. I was to wait three months for my pay, it being in the fall, I thought I should not want my money before March, when I expected to start for Georgia.

I then hired with a man by the name of Kincade; he was a stranger, just come into the neighborhood and had rented a farm that was considerably out of repair, and he wanted a smart chance of work done. He was a man of very fair speech and had a wife that was a dead match for himself. I hired with them to make rails by the hundred, without any definite number being specified, which gave me a chance to quit when I pleased. I went to work and labored hard, in order to make as good wages as possible. The old man, in the meantime, fell in love with my gun, and every night made proposals to purchase; I did not like to part with her, but at last concluded I had no great use for her, nor had I time to spend in shooting. I sold her to the old man, who was to pay me at the time that the other was to pay for my horse.

I worked on for about three weeks, in which time I had made twenty-five hundred rails. The old man did not seem to care about working much himself. He had been married to his second wife and had had five children by his first. His present wife did not appear to be very young or beautiful, and seemed as though, in the tempering, she had been cast into the water while very hot.

There was a still-house within about a mile of us, and the old man attended pretty regularly with his jug. When he brought it home, his wife, in great good humor, would join in with him, and turned up her little finger as often as he, and neither appeared disposed to give much away, so that by the time supper was over, (which was always after night,) instead of psalm singing there was considerable swearing to be done, at which I thought the woman was the hardest hand. I had been taught to believe it was wrong for a woman to swear, and I think yet it adds nothing to the charms of beautiful woman, nor do I commend it in a man. I always went to bed soon after supper, and when they got their steam well up, would sit up late, and I would at times hear some unpleasant remarks made about the children; when both got warm the old woman could rather head the man, until she got his mettle up, then she was compelled to knock under. I began to get a little tired of the place and proposed to the old man to be off. When we came to settle he could not pay me for my labor, which I expected down; he gave fair promises. I then went to a man named Alison, with whom I was acquainted. He agreed to hire me through the winter, if I chose to stay, and if I did not, I was at liberty to leave when I saw proper. He had one son about my age and another older; we had been raised together, in the same neighborhood. Here I was very agreeably situated, for there was neither psalm singing, drinking whiskey nor swearing, but plenty of hard work to do all day, and the boys and I went a coon-hunting almost every night.

I was very well situated, and expected to stay all winter; I had a sister married, who was living in Georgia, and about Christmas times, she and her husband came on a visit to my father's. My father and brother-in-law came to where I was working; I dropped my tools, and went home with them. After consulting on matters, I concluded to fix up, and go to Georgia with my sister. Having but a short time to make arrangements, I went to my last employer, Alison, and told him my intention; he paid me without hesitation. I then went to my first one, but he did not seem so willing to see me; the time had not elapsed that he had to pay me for my colt, and did not wish to suffer any inconvenience; he would not give me my colt again, although I offered to pay for his keeping; neither had he the money, he said, to pay me. I was compelled to have some kind of a horse, give out my journey, or take it on foot; at length, he agreed, that if I could get a horse that would suit me, on a credit, that he would be responsible. I knew his responsibility was good. I went to an old neighbors of my fathers, by the name of Walsh, who had a snug pony, that I thought would answer, and made him proposals. The old man did not wish to part with his pony, but let me have him, more from an accommodation, I believed, than from a wish to sell. In this matter I lost considerable, for my colt was worth two such ponies. I then went to my friend Kincade, but found I had but a slim chance of getting any thing for my gun and labor; money was out of the question; the thing that I most needed. At length, he proposed, that if I would go with him to a little kind of store that was in the neighborhood, and take some articles, he would pay me. Thinking that something was better than nothing, I went, and got a very few articles at a very high price—

but few of them suited me. Another sister took a notion to go with my married sister, and there were some arrangements to make for that purpose. We got all things ready, and bid farewell to Carolina. My sister had a bed and several articles she needed, and I some clothing to carry; therefore, it became necessary to pack one horse, and in consequence thereof, I and my brother-in-law had to walk, time about, most part of the way. I had no previous knowledge of this brother-in-law, or what kind of a man he was; but I found him, afterwards, to be one of the best of men—as true and firm a friend as I ever had. This was, if I recollect right, in January, 1785.

We pursued our journey without much difficulty and arrived safe at the residence of my brother-in-law. I had expended the most of what little money I had, and must therefore do something to reimburse my purse. After resting a few days, and endeavoring how to consult my best interests, I luckily found out there was a man who had moved from the neighborhood of my father's whom I had known almost all my life, by the name of Fergus. He was a man of business habits and had become popular in the country and the appointment of Surveyor had been given him. He lived some miles higher up the country than where my sister lived. Fergus's residence was one of the outside houses on the frontier. I went to see him and explained the object of my visit; after some consultation on the subject, he advised me, first to get a land warrant, have the land surveyed, obtain a grant—teach a country school for a few months—and that he would assist me in so doing.

CHAPTER XI.

VARIOUS OCCUPATIONS.

I COULD then write a pretty fair hand, and also, knew something of reading, and arithmetic. I took the advice of Fergus, and got a school of twenty-five scholars for three months, at one dollar per head, for each scholar, and my board; in the bargain. I fulfilled my time, and got most of my pay without any trouble; I was urged a little to continue, but did not like the business; it was too confining, and I thought I could make more by joining in with some of the surveyors; I wanted to see the country; I agreed with Mr. Fergus to go as a chain bearer. We would often be out some fifteen or twenty days; it required four to do the surveying, and we generally had two or more to go along as hunters, to keep us in provisions; and, sometimes, there would be with us, "land hunters."

I found a piece of land that was vacant, that I thought would suit me. I went to the land court and obtained what was called a head right warrant, for two hundred acres, and had it located. I discovered there was an abundance of game in the woods; I became fond of the idea of hunting, and to that end, I got me a good rifle. I knew how to shoot pretty well, but knew little of hunting, and found, that it required some experience. Deer and turkies were very plenty; also, bear, panthers, wild cats, foxes, and many other wild animals. I turned my attention rather too much to hunting and became almost as fond of the sport as David Crocket, but never was near a match for him at a bear hunt. I frequently went with the surveying companies, and generally chose to become one of the hunters; thus I became a good woodsman, and also became acquainted with all the water courses on the frontier of Georgia.

After the lands were mostly surveyed, and vacant land that was good not easily found, a great many young men that came to the country, and were entitled to head rights, would sell their warrants for very trifling sums. I shifted about until I bought three, and my knowledge of the country enabled me to find lands on which to locate my warrants, so that I became the owner of four tracts, containing two hundred acres each, in different parts. When I was not in the woods, I worked hard.

In the fall of 1788, if my memory serves me, a draft of two thousand militia was ordered, to guard a treaty to be made with the Creek Indians, for the Saxmulgee lands. I stood my draft, and drew a blank; there were numbers that did not wish to go and were eager to hire substitutes; among others, I hired as a substitute, and went. We were marched to a place called Shoulderbone, on a creek running into the Oconee, and about a mile from the river. The Indians encamped on the side opposite to us. We commenced building store houses, to secure the provisions, and a house for the council. Around the Council House was enclosed a square, of perhaps an acre, with a strong high fence, and a large gate, to pass in and out. The buildings being finished, the parade ground was cleaned out in front of the lines. When the council commenced, there was a strong guard of horsemen, to conduct the Indians to and from their encampment, and a guard at the ford to prevent the whites from crossing over to the Indian camp. There was also a strong guard placed every morning in the enclosure around the Council House, to prevent any one from passing in and out to disturb the council. Here I was appointed drum major, and had little to do, not being liable to work, or stand on duty. Here we lay, until we began to get somewhat gay—having little to do but eat. Our commissaries had bought a good deal of new corn meal, which began to sour and become unpalatable; they kept dealing it out, although there was plenty of flour and good meal in store; but I suppose they thought the bad meal would be a dead loss, when they could dispose of the good to advantage, by furnishing the Indians therewith. We complained to our officers, and they applied to some of the heads of the department for better meal, but there was little attention paid to their application. We seemed to be divided into two classes; the upper, denominated Highlanders; those of the low country, Lowlanders. Most of the Lowlanders, were sick and weakly looking fellows, while the Highlanders were healthy, stout, and frolicsome. The Highlanders were encamped at the head of the lines, near head quarters.

One clear, moonlight night, a number began to parade, each man taking a brush on his shoulder instead of a gun, and commenced marching backwards and forwards along the lines, to have a frolic, and making a great deal of noise they marched up to headquarters, and formed a circle around the quarter master's tent, and demanded better meal for the future, and also their rations of rum, that had been kept back for several days, threatening to take it by force unless their demands were complied with. Being sharply reprimanded and threatened with arrest and punishment, they marched back and told the news. Almost immediately, the whole line of Highlanders were paraded, and each man shouldering a branch of a tree cut from the parade ground, commenced their march up the lines; their motion was noticed and the horsemen, who lay at some distance, were called in. The march continued until we had gone round headquarters, without interrupting any one or anything, and were returning to our quarters, when suddenly the horsemen passed across the parade ground before us, ordering us to stand and throw down our branches. The word was instantly given by our leaders, to charge; it was obeyed with a general shout; in a few minutes most of the horsemen were thrown from their horses, and run over by the crowd. However, they took five or six prisoners that had become entangled in some brush. All went to their tents, except the horsemen who were kept on guard all night. Early next morning there was a considerable stir in camp, and some of the officers who had conducted the affair of the night previous, were along the lines, advising us not to recede, and some of the other officers joined in. Very soon, almost the whole line of Highlanders was paraded under arms; a flag was sent, demanding the prisoners, intimating in case of non-compliance, they would be taken by force, and we would forthwith march off the ground. The proposition was at first rejected and the dispute became very warm between some of the officers; at last our principal leader came galloping down, and ordered us to shoulder our knapsacks, and be ready to march. The most of the Lowlanders lay neutral in their tents, like good fellows. Their principal officer refusing to interfere, and several horsemen turned over to our side, alleging they had been imposed upon in the same way. At length three or four of the principal officers, Gen Triggs for one, came riding down the lines and mildly told us to return to our tents, like good fellows, and they would release the prisoners, and we should have good provisions for the future. This was enough; all consented, and harmony was restored. It began without any serious intention of mischief and so was more easily quieted. I merely mention this circumstance to show what unruly cattle a set of militia-men are, when they have nothing to do. After lying here something over two months, the business was concluded and we were all discharged, and returned home.

 In the course of the summer preceeding this treaty, the Cherokee Indians had been somewhat troublesome, on the frontier, and caused the people to gather into forts for safety; men were called on to guard the forts and among others I was drafted to serve a twenty days' tour. I went to a fort on

Broad River, at a place called Skull Shoal. The weather was very warm, and I, among others, was a little imprudent about going into the water when warm. I took a fever and had to be carried home; there were no physicians in the country near; I was unaccustomed to physic, or fever, it being the first severe attack of the kind I ever had. Neither did I ever have the shaking ague, although raised in a country where it was prevalent every season; I had a high fever for four or five days without intermission. At length it was advised by some to bleed me freely in the feet in order to bring on a shaking ague which I have thought since was a rash proceeding. I submitted and the operation was performed—I was bled plentifully from the feet. It had the desired effect by bringing on a severe shake, which continued, daily for nine weeks. The shake would come on about noon every day, then a fever ensue, and about midnight sweat off. In the morning I was up and about my business until the shake returned. After having the shakes some days, my appetite for food became good and indeed rather too much so. All this time I took no medicine but simple teas prescribed by some old woman. I got very tired of my ague and began to conclude I was never going to get clear of it. Some would advise me to do one thing and some another, by way of charm or spell, but to tell the truth, I had no faith in any such things. At length some one assured me that if I would prepare a string long enough to tie as many knots as I had had shakes, and when I felt the shakes coming on, take my string and go to some fruit bearing tree, turn my back and put my string around the tree, and counting, tie a knot for every shake including the one coming on, and depart without looking back, it would cure me. I own I had no faith in the project, neither would I recommend it to any one, yet I thought there could be no harm in it; I tried it, and my shake coming on, it was as much as I could do to hold out, having sixty-three knots to tie. I had fatigued myself, and my shake was severer than common; but be that as it may the thing did not return.

CHAPTER XII.

SCENES AND ADVENTURES.

EARLY in the summer of 1790, the Cherokee and Creek Indians both broke out, and became very troublesome all along the line of the frontier, on the two sides of Georgia, so as to cause all the inhabitants there residing, to betake themselves to forts, and the militia were called out to guard the forts. Among others, I was drafted to serve a twenty day's tour; the next draft, I took hire as a substitute. It became necessary to have spies, in order to discover, if possible, the approach of the Indians. There was a Captain William Black, who had been raised in the country, had been through the revolutionary war, and was well acquainted with the manners and customs of the Indians. He was chosen, at the fort where I was, to ride as a spy. He and I had hunted a good deal together, and he chose that I should go with him; we had a line of near twenty miles to ride, including four forts, which took us nearly three days to make our trip and return, always having to camp out one night. In starting out, we made it a rule to travel out several miles, in order to avoid the cattle range. so that we might discover any trail that might be passing in. I was little acquainted with the customs of the Indians, and was compelled to be guided by my companion.— We were under pay for our services, and so concluded to stay as long as we might be needed. We always carried provisions for ourselves and horses. Two trips had been made without our making any discovery; on the third, we started out very early in the morning and travelled nearly all day without making any discovery; late in the evening we struck a fresh trail making in towards the settlements. It appeared from the sign that there was a pretty smart company of Indians; we followed the trail with caution, until we came to a small creek; they had waded through the creek and the water was still in their tracks. As soon as Black discovered that, he clapped spurs to his horse, saying: "There's no time to be lost here." I followed; we rode briskly on until we got on to high, open ground; then halted, and took a view all round. My companion then observed, "We are in a ticklish place; for it is quite probable that these Indians have discovered us, for they cannot be far off, and if so, they will try to trail us up and catch us in the night." The sun was near setting, and it was impossible for us to get into the settlement or fort; we got upon the highest open ridge we could find, and keeping a good lookout, moved on until the dusk of the evening. We stopped and he pointed out a course which he directed me to take with both horses, and go on some three or four hundred yards, then stop and set down both corn bags and open them, then let the horses eat, but not to unbit the bridles, to keep my gun in my hand and be ready in a moment, in case I should hear him coming, haste to tie the bags, and be ready to mount, that he would way-lay the trail perhaps till some time after dark, if no danger appeared. I obeyed, and went on until I thought I had gone far enough, opened the bags and put the horses to feeding, standing off a short distance and listened attentively. I had not waited long before I heard Black coming in a run; by the time the bags were tied he had come up; each one threw up his bag and mounted. The Indians, I suppose, had discovered him, and when he run, pursued. By the time we were fairly in our saddles, the Indians were within a short distance—I thought thirty yards, but perhaps the distance was greater. There was no time for counting and it was too dark to guess at numbers. We dashed off at full speed. The horse that my companion rode was a very spirited, strong one and blind in one eye; at a short distance from where we started, there was a large fallen pine, with a heavy top. It had probably been down some time, so that the branches had commenced rotting; the fright perhaps, and he putting spurs to his horse caused him suddenly to dash in among the branches of the tree, with a great crashing for a moment or two, and I was really afraid he would be entangled until the Indians would be upon us, but he came out safe. The woods being very open, we rode fast for some three or four miles, then halted and listened awhile but heard nothing. We changed our course, and took two or three short tacks; again we stopped, sat on our horses some time, and no danger appearing, dismounted, stirpped our horses and tied them fast to two saplings. Moving our saddles and provisions some distance from our horses, and taking our guns we went off with caution for some distance, and laid down upon the grass. We were near enough together to watch each other, and be able to speak in case of any noise; we laid perfectly still, without any idea of sleeping until fair daylight in the morning. As soon as it was light enough to see plainly, we arose and took a view all around. Seeing our horses standing safe, we took a circle round, keeping at a distance from them. Asking his motive for this manœuvre, he told me that we were in the enemy's country, and they were in the woods near us, and we had been discovered; that there might be more than one company, and we, riding in the night might be discovered, by another; that on search being made by them in the night, and our horses found, they would know that we were not far distant, and to make sure of us they would lie in ambush near the horses. Advising me at the same time, if we should be attacked, it would be imprudent to discharge both guns at the same time, but to retreat as well as possible keeping close together, and if we were too closely pursued, to stop and take trees; on presenting our guns, they would immediately fall to the ground, which would give us a chance for a new start. Unless they are numerous, they will not charge fiercely on two men with loaded guns. We made our circle, but saw nothing; we then went to our horses; all was safe; we saddled up in a hurry, got our provisions, and started.— After riding some distance, we alighted, fed our horses, and took something to eat ourselves, for we were hungry, having eaten nothing the night before. I would here remark, that it is an invariable rule with an Indian, when once discovered, to give over all further pursuit of his object for the present. My companion seemed to be aware of this, so that we kept on our route, without returning to the fort to give the alarm.

As soon as the fall season approached, the Indians always gave up their depredations, and all was peace, until the return of summer, when they would repeat their former acts, and so continue to do until its close. During the fall and winter, most of the families would leave the forts, go home and attend to their affairs, until the Indians broke out the next summer. As soon as it was peaceable, I would return to the settlement, and go to hard labor during winter and spring. I could use the axe, maul and wedges, or mattock, as well as most men, and I preferred exercise to sedentary habits. There was a cooper worked at the place where I generally made my home, and in bad weather, or at any idle time, I was always in the shop at work, by which means I learned to make a pretty good rough vessel. Jumping, running and wrestling, were very fashionable in those times; these I practised very often, and though not one of the first class, I rated pretty well in the second.

CHAPTER XIII.

THE SPRING OF 1791. THE INDIANS.

DEPREDATIONS by the Indians, were again commenced, in the spring, or rather summer, of 1791. They committed more murders and stole more horses, than they did the summer preceding. It is not common for Indians, unless in considerable force, to attack in broad day-light, a fort, or place, guarded by a number of men. On the contrary, they always choose the twilight of the evening, or the morning, before sunrise—but so it was. There was a fort called Bridge's Fort ; it stood on high ground. In front was an open field, in which stood a large mulberry tree ;— the tree was full of fruit, and the fruit was ripe. The proprietor, one day before noon, concluded he would have some of the fruit; thinking of no danger, he took his gun, and taking with him his son, a small lad, he went to the tree ; setting down his gun by its side, he climbed up, and shook down the fruit.— While his little son was gathering it up, the Indians, unperceived, got near enough to shoot the man out of the tree, taking the little boy prisoner, and commencing an attack upon the fort, which lasted for some time. At length, being unsuccessful in their attack, they marched off with their prisoner, the gun, and the unfortunate man's scalp. A runner had got out of the fort at the commencement, and the alarm soon spread. By sunrise, next morning, there were about two hundred men, at the fort, all under arms, exclusive of the guard belonging to the fort. Leaving a small guard, about two hundred men turned out to pursue the enemy; we took their trail and followed them; we crossed one prong of the Oconee River, finding the signs very fresh, and that the number of Indians had increased. We went on six or seven miles, keeping spies a little ahead, my friend Black being one. On crossing an open ridge, three Indians appeared in front at a distance on the trail. The spies fell back and reported. We then prepared for an attack. There was a large creek just ahead called Barber's Creek, and a thick canebreak.

As soon as we were nearly in gun-shot of the cane, we were ordered to wheel to the right, and leave the trail, keeping up the creek a small distance, where our woodsmen assured us there was an open crossing place. This drew the Indians out of the cane into a kind of brushwood on our left, to prevent us, I suppose, from crossing. They attacked us: we were in much more open ground than they, so that they came up pretty close, making all the hideous yells that they were masters of. The contest lasted warmly for about an hour—I thought much longer at the time. During the action, a man by the name of Ashworth, and myself kept close together; we both took one tree. A very small tree will cover a man's body in front if he stands right. We had discharged our guns; two balls had struck the tree where we stood and knocked the bark off; there was a bunch of brush and vines, nearly in front of us, and we had both noticed the smoke rise from a gun in this place, but saw no object. We shifted quickly to another tree at a small distance on our left, and discovered an Indian on his knees loading his gun. Our guns being loaded, we both leveled and fired, nearly at the same time; the fellow keeled over and lay still; he was too near us for his friends to remove him, I think not more than forty steps, so that when the fight was decided we got his scalp and gun. One ball had struck him right in the breast, and the other had broken his collar bone. After a hard and obstinate fight, the Indians fled and we had four fine fellows killed, and if I recollect right, fourteen or fifteen wounded, but none mortally. How many Indians we killed it was impossible to tell. We got ten scalps, and found by the blood where a number had been taken off. It is an Indian custom to take off all their dead that they can possibly get at, with any degree of safety. I suppose we got the fellow who scalped the man killed at the fort, for we got the scalp and the gun, but not the little boy, though he was afterwards given up. We buried our poor fellows as well as we could, and got our wounded all safe home, where they recovered in a short time.

It will be remembered that these were a party of Creek Indians. Capt. Black and myself were again induced to ride as spies on our old route. This was on the Cherokee line, and we had made two trips without making any discovery. On the third trip, one morning before we had ridden far we fell on a trail that made in towards the settlements. The people were mostly at home, careless. We took the trail and followed on until the Indians all scattered. Here, I would again remark that the Indians, when they intend doing mischief, and come in any force, as soon as they are near the settlement where they intend to strike, they disperse in order to avoid discovery and meet at a place appointed, near where they intend committing their depredation; as soon as we discovered they had scattered, we pushed on with all speed for the settlement, to give the alarm. As soon as we got in, the news spread, and almost every family fled to the fort for safety, leaving most of their plunder behind.

There was one family living within four miles of the fort, a widow by the name of Crockett, having one son and five daughters, all grown. The young women were of high respectability, and considered the handsomest in the whole country, so that numbers of the young men interested themselves in giving them all the assistance in their power, and several called in, in the course of the evening for the purpose of urging them to go, and also to assist them. But they refused and alleged it was a false alarm ; that there had been several alarms when there was no danger, and they would not go in until the next day. So they were left to their own will, to risk it until morning. Early next morning three or four started from the fort to see the result and help them in. But doleful to tell!—when they got to the place, every one lay stretched in the yard, a corpse, scalped and mangled in the most shocking manner imaginable, and every article of clothing and bedding taken away and the feathers of the bed strown all over the yard.

The news soon came to the fort; we collected all the force we could, pursued, but could not overtake them ; they crossed the Chattahoochee river, and dispersed. It was impossible to trail them any further—besides, we were in their country, and not far distant from some of their towns—not having force sufficient, nor provisions ;—but we paid them for it afterwards.— They committed several other murders, in the course of the summer, near the same place. In order to chastise them, about the time their corn was in full roasting ears, there was a company of men raised and started out to their town. There was a town called Long Swamp, that was blamed for most of the mischief. My friend Black and myself were in the company ; we steered our course for the Long Swamp, and having good pilots, we were in the town, right among the Indians, before we were discovered—and here it was, helter skelter among them, who should get off fastest, without offering to give us battle.— Few escaped ; men, women, and children were killed ; a few small Indian boys were taken prisoners by some of our men who thought they could make slaves of them, but in this they found themselves mistaken ; for after a trial of four or five years, they could make nothing of them but Indians, and sent them back to the nation.

Here I must mention a little circumstance about my friend Black. After killing the Indians that could be found, the men began to fire the town ; there was a house shut up, and Black, suspecting there was some Indians in it, attempted to force the door, but finding it not easily done, with his loaded gun in his hand, sprung up on the roof, thinking to open a hole therein and shoot down, as soon as he mounted. The timbers being rotten, the roof gave way, and down went Black into the middle of the house ; when he landed, there was an old squaw and some children ; the old squaw charged on him immediately with her hatchet ; in too close quarters to shoot, he closed in with her and called for help. It was some seconds before the door could be forced, but when done, Black was found in close hug with the old woman, she still retaining her hatchet, trying to strike him. After firing the town, we next cut down the corn, thus leaving the place a heap of ruins.

We had many little chases after the Indians but of small consequence—I shall mention but one or two more. The Creek Indians came in and attacked a fort, early in the morning. Just before daylight, in the morning, two men went out some distance to look a shoal in the river for deer, and on their return got among the Indians. At that instant the firing commenced ; the men tried to make their way to the fort, but were discovered and prevented, some of the Indians being between them and the fort. Another party was firing on the cowpens, where some of the women had gone out to milk. The men fled and some of the Indians pursued, while the others kept up a firing on the fort. The Indians in pursuit had fired several guns, while the two men, when too closely pursued would take trees and present their guns. The Indians would fall flat to the ground. After running some considerable distance, a shot from one of the Indians struck one of the men, in the leg, just above the ankle, and passed up the hind part of the leg, just below the knee, but without affecting the bone. He still run on, being protected by the other, who would turn, present his gun and thus stop the Indians until his companion could get another start. After running on in this way for near a mile, they got to a canebreak which they entered and found a small stream of water. The wounded man lay down in the stream where he was covered all over but his head, and the other left for the settlement expecting that the fort had been taken. He had at least six or seven miles to run, to get to the nearest house. The alarm spread fast, so that early in the afternoon there were two hundred men at the fort; but behold the business was all over—the Indians were gone and all was still, and no damage done, only the one man wounded. The first care was to hunt him up, which was done after his companion got back to the fort. In the meantime, all the people in the fort, had given them both up for lost. When we found him, the poor fellow had nearly given himself up for lost, thinking the fort taken, and perhaps the people all murdered, and was afraid to crawl out for fear of being caught. He stated, the Indians in searching for him, had crossed the stream in which he lay, on a log, so near him that he could see the rings in their ears. At the same time he had two dogs lying near him, and though usually fierce, lay perfectly still and never even growled, as if conscious that his fate depended on their keeping quiet. This seemed an interposition of divine providence.

It was proposed to raise a company and pursue after the Indians; the inhabitants of the fort presuming that there was not more than twenty-five or thirty that had attacked them. In order to raise a company, there were two captains turned out; one named McClaskey, and the other, Howell. McClaskie had been a captain in the Revolution, on the frontier of South Carolina, and was acquainted with the nature of the Indian warfare; the other, Howell, was a young man, just got into office, no doubt of sufficient courage, but lacking experience, and a little rash. Each captain soon raised fifteen men, in all thirty; they were deemed sufficient for the pursuit. For my own part, I turned out with McClaskey; we made sufficient search to discover the trail they had taken that evening, and next morning commenced an early pursuit; we followed on two days, and on the third, early in the morning, we crossed the Apalache river. Some two or three miles after crossing, the signs became very fresh, and appeared like the number of Indians had increased very considerably. It was proposed to call a halt and hold a counsel. This was done; McClaskey advised a return, alleging that from every appearance, the enemy was vastly superior; that we were in the enemy's country and that no doubt they were aware, of our approach and number; the first thing we would know, we would be drawn into an ambuscade, and perhaps every man killed; and he thought it not right to urge men into danger where there was not the least probability of success. Howell insisted on proceeding at all hazards, saying he was determined to have a fight before he returned, if only five men would stand by him. At length both the officers got a little warm on the subject, and some unpleasant words passed between them. Each one stepped out, leaving it to the men to follow whom they chose. McClaskey's men all followed him, and five of Howell's. Howell then made some remarks rather branding his men with cowardice. There is something in man that cannot well brook the name of coward although he may really feel something of the effect. They were all young, vigorous, and full of life and action, but entirely unacquainted with the Indian disposition, and scarce one of them had even seen an Indian in a hostile attitude. At length the men belonging to each company followed their leader and we parted. We, the retreating party steered our course for home as fast as we could. We got home, or into the settlement, and on the evening of the following day, two of Howell's men came into the fort, one of them shot through the fleshy part of the thigh. They stated that they had proceeded about four or five miles, from where we separated, and the thing had taken place just as McClaskey had predicted, and that the probabilty was that the others were all killed. Poor fellows,—it proved too true ! The same officer and two others then raised a pretty strong company, and pushed on with all speed, to learn the certainty, and bury the dead, if we could find them. We got to the place, and beheld a melancholy and distressing sight. It would seem from every appearance, that twelve of the men had fallen at the first fire for they all lay within a small space of ground, tomahawked and scalped—several balls had passed through some of them. As for Capt. Howell, three balls had passed through his body, and one had broken his arm. The other four had attempted to escape, and had run perhaps three or four hundred yards from the place where they were overtaken, and two killed, and one of the others received his wound, as he afterwards stated.

We deposited the remains of our poor unfortunate comrades in the earth, the best we could, which was by no means a pleasant business, for they had now been dead, above four days. I have often wondered why they had not been torn by wild beasts in the time. We could account for it no other way than the strong smell of gunpowder, that was on them, and no rain having fallen on them in the time.

CHAPTER XIV.

RELIGIOUS VIEWS—DANCING AND SINGING SCHOOLS—HUNTING.

I NOW retired pretty much from the forts and fell into other business. There was an old Dutchman, with whom I had some acquaintance, who kept a tailor shop, and to improve myself in the business, I joined in with him to work as a journeyman. The old man was remarkably fond of horses, and was thought a good judge; and horse trading began to be quite a business in the country. As there was not work enough to keep us busy, the Dutchman paid a good deal of attention to the horse trading business, and encouraged me to join him in it. I was by no means averse to it, being fond of horses myself. I acquired considerable insight respecting the diseases, ages and forms of horses, from the Dutchman, and some other horse traders from North Carolina, Virginia and other places, with whom we had correspondence; also the treatment necessary for horses in different stages. Before I dismiss my Dutchman, I must remark that he taught me several little Dutch tricks, that not many persons believe, which in themselves are simple, yet a little curious. There was, also, an old Dutch lady lived in the neighborhood who even surpassed the old man; for some of her feats I cannot to this day account. About this time, preaching began to be popular among the people, which had been for several year neglected, as is usual in almost all new settled countries. For when people have to labor hard, live hard—and that on coarse food, and wear ragged clothes—

they have little to spare, and it is hardly worth while for preachers, lawyers, doctors or dancing masters to attend to their case, until they get, at least, one suit of clothing and other things in proportion; and I even think we might besides those, include our legislators, and those connected in the great sanhedrim of our nation. They have some little delicacies about them that will not bear rough handling, and look for some other delicacies—eating, lodging and apparel—and above all they like to be furnished with a pretty good share of money. But to do justice to the doctors, I must confess I have always found them to be the most liberal and humane of any professional men with whom I have been compelled to have any intercourse. To the lawyers, I have been under few obligations, and feel willing to excuse them measurably, believing they generally act up to their profession; but the priests—with a number of whom I have been acquainted and had some intercourse— with a few exceptions, I have always found to be illiberal, and have been more exposed to their contempt than pity, because I could not assent to every creed that they proposed, nor obey all their mandates; neither did I find myself able or willing to advance as much money to their support as they adjudged I ought to do for the neglect of which duties as they called them and the doctrines they advance, in support of such duties, is that a man might be inevitably damned. I will hereafter perhaps mention some circumstances, which gave rise to the above remarks. I made it a point to attend church regularly on Sundays, and often on other days of the week. Not being a member of any particular church, I attended any that was most convenient. There was a considerable revival in religion, and we had a number of preachers of different denominations—Presbyterians, Baptists, Methodists, and once in a while a Universalian, and being under no obligation to any particular sect, I attended all as circumstances suited. Perhaps through the prejudices of education and some early impressions, rather enforced on my mind in youth, I inclined a little more to the Presbyterians than any other sect. I thought them more liberal in matters of conscience, notwithstanding I thought their leaders by far too rigid in many things, and not doubting they preferred the fleece to the real health of the flock yet they seemed to avow it more openly, and seemed willing to inculcate the principle and even enforce it on their hearers while others denied the principle but strenuously recommended free-will offerings which I thought implied the same thing only under a cloak.

I am willing to admit a few exceptions, but at the same time taking in the whole, that it is like all mechanical trades, money is the principal object. Here you might think I was about to cry down all religion : far from it! that there is religion and that it is essential to the comfort and happiness of mankind in general, and to every community, there can be no doubt, with every thinking man. For without it no community can be happy or prosperous, but this religion does not consist in little ceremonies and formalities belonging to the different churches, or in this or that particular church, nor in believing everything your preacher says, because he tells you he believes it. As self interest is prevalent among all classes of men, so I am apt to think the preachers are not exempt; the social friendly, honest, man, that acts from pure motives, that renders justice to all to the extent of his power, that renders to every one that which under the same circumstances, he would wish others to render unto him—it is he who fulfils the great plan of nature. That there is a God, the great Creator and Controller of universal nature, that the most elevated conceptions of man, can form no adequate idea of, only through his own mysterious works, and that he made all things according to his own wisdom —to fulfil his own purposes ; and I think few will deny, that we receive all the blessings of life from that exalted being and that it is the duty of all, to worship him as the author of our being, and of all our enjoyment. For my own part, I readily grant the right to preach up religion and morality, for doubtless morality is a concomitant of religion, but to bind down the consciences of men in points of faith and modes of worship, because it is your belief, or in case he refuses, consign him over to eternal damnation is too intolerant and unfits a man for being a good parent, husband, citizen or patriot. I think there is nothing more opposed to patriotism than intolerance in religious creeds. I would take this maxim : here is freedom to him that would read, here is freedom to him that would write, here is freedom to him that would think, and farther, the thinking faculty of man is uncontrolable, for it is absolutely not under his control, much less that of another and of course must go free in spite of all efforts to control it. As all the preachers pretend to ape St. Paul, and take him for their standard, if they would pursue the same course and determine to preach Jesus Christ and him crucified, and lay aside their little sectarian principles, and unite all their forces to accomplish the design on which they all say they have set out, viz: the happiness of man, I think it would show a more patriotic and republican spirit. Making so many roads all starting from the same place, and all terminating at the same place, and all for the very same purpose and the hands working on the different routes, eternally abusing and insulting each other, about their modes of worshiping, the materials they use, the kind of tools they work with, and their clothing and diet also called in question and even their mode of sleeping and taking nourishment on the way is often found fault with. If they would concentrate all their forces and make one common cause of it, and set all the laborers on the same road, I think the united efforts of all would make a better way with less labor, and keep in repair with more ease, and travelers would find ease and safety, in passing the road ; there would be fewer toll bridges, necessary to be kept up on the way, than on the present plan, if the rulers instead of being harsh drivers and hard taskmasters would take the lead in the work, and put themselves as near as might be on a par with the common laborers and by industry and patience set a good example and not claim as is customary enormous salaries and perhaps ten or twelve rations a day, and that of the very best the community affords; but, without laying a finger to the work they stand aloof and issue orders in the most peremptory manner, under the severest penalties; and if a poor fellow that is no great mechanic and has labored but little in the business, happens to bore an auger hole a little crooked or perhaps cuts his leg a little with the foot adze, they will not only turn him off the road but pack him off straight to hell without the least chance of redemption. There is a sense of right and wrong implanted in the breast of every man, and he that does justice, loves mercy and walks humbly before God, according to the best of his powers, I would respect as a religious man whether he belongs to any particular church or not, or whether there is any particular ceremony attached to his creed, or mode of worship. To force a man to believe a thing because I believe it, or to enforce any religious creed on another man's conscience when perhaps I hardly believe it myself, only for the sake of becoming popular, is not consistent with true republican principle. If honest nature made a man a fool I believe it is out of the power of man to make him wise.

I think old Solomon discovered that in his time, if God made man a fool, he would require but little at his hands for his lack of knowledge. The most of men have some reasoning faculties, and if another man after reasoning on the subject, cannot view religious matters in the same light that you do it is unfair to condemn him. God only knows the purity of the motive, and he neither needs or wants the assistance of man to sit in judgment. But, enough of this digression. so I will turn to my subject.

So at the same time, there were several dancing masters in almost every quarter. Notwithstanding the revival in religion, dancing masters got sufficient encouragement, for dancing was very fashionable among the people. I was immoderately fond of music and dancing, so I made it a point to attend dancing school pretty often. There was another fashion prevalent at this time; so soon as winter approached, every woman in the country that wanted a little cotton for spinning would invite all her neighbors, old and young, to help her pick some cotton of a night; at that time there were no gins in the country. In consequence of their picking a smart chance of cotton, they were entitled to the privilege of a dance; after they had finished their task of cotton, and got supper, the dance commenced, and seldom ceased until daylight next morning. I was too fond of the business to let such opportunities slip, so I frequently attended on such occasions. I was so fond of it that I determined to become a fiddler; to that end I bought a fiddle, for which, after having her adjudged by a dancing master, I gave three hundred pounds of leaf tobacco, which was selling for from three to five dollars per hundred weight. I commenced practicing on my fiddle, at all leisure hours, but to my mortification, after making sufficient experiment I discovered I could not perform to my wish—I could tune the instrument well enough, but I never could note to please myself, consequently I concluded that I could not please others that were judges. My fingers were too contracted at the ends, and would always touch in playing; I thought if I could not perform, equal to the best, that I would not practice at all, so I laid aside the instrument.

About this time also, singing masters, as they are called, began to come into the country. I was fond of music any way, and having been taught something of vocal music in early life, I attended those schools under the tuition of what was called good teachers. There were two of the most noted, one by the name of Neel and the other, Mays, who acted in concert, and whose school I mostly attended; sometimes, others, that were not so good. I continued this practice, until I commenced teaching myself, which I practiced a number of years; of this, I may say more hereafter.

As my attendance at church or the schools I have spoken of, seldom required more than two days in the week—say Saturday and Sunday—sometimes, not so much. I was mostly employed in some kind of labor—and few came round that I did not understand. I could use an axe, mattock, or maul and wedges, and in this few could head me; I was good at the plow—a work I delighted in—or at at the hoe; I could weave, make shoes, cooper, or work in the tailor shop; I could use some carpenters' tools pretty well, and whatever business suited best I worked at. Whenever the first hard frosts set in, in the fall, I always shouldered my gun and put off to the woods with some hunting party; the best hunting season generally lasted about two months. Game of different kinds was plenty, and peltry was bringing a good price; deer skins were worth twenty-five cents per pound, and other skins sold according to quality; and all were as good as cash in any of the stores. The rule in hunting, was for each man belonging to the company to draw an equal share of the meat, whether successful in hunting or not, while each one kept all the skins he took. For my own part, I generally pursued the deer, which was the most plentiful game, and their skins the most profitable. I have frequently killed five in a day, and sometimes more, and when the weather was unfavorable, I have often hunted diligently all day, and killed but one or two, and sometimes, but seldom, killed none during a hard day's hunt. I have often killed old bucks that one single hide would weigh twelve pounds, but I do not recollect more than twelve or fifteen that I ever killed, of that weight, that I weighed separately. It requires some judgment in skinning and stretching to make skins pass well in market. The average weight of good skins is from six to eight pounds. I have frequently in my hunting, killed foxes, raccoons, wild cats and sometimes a panther; turkies we seldom killed, when camped out, hunting, except for our own use, as they are hard to keep from spoiling. Bears were tolerably plenty, but our bear hunts did not come on until about the close of the fall —at which time, the trapping season for furs, also commenced. Although I was hard to match at a deer hunt, yet I was not so good after a bear though fond of the sport. Among all my companions in hunting for deer, I never found but one man who I thought was an overmatch for me in the same woods. I could find as many deer as any man, but in killing he was a full match, if not better than myself. I always thought it was owing to the circumstance of his shooting at more risk, for he would shoot let the chances be good or bad, while I always tried to make a pretty sure shot, and by that means lost many chances. Bear hunting was attended with more fatigue, than any other, for their haunts were always in rougher ground and often attended with some danger, but when fat their meat was thought valuable. It always requires more than one to manage a bear hunt well. The largest one I ever assisted in killing, after the hide was taken off, the entrails taken out, the head and feet taken off, and divided into quarters, weighed a little over nine hundred pounds. All that I made by my share of the meat, of any kind, was barely the amusement of hunting it. I had a brother and sister, both older than myself who lived in the neighborhood and had families. I divided my meat for the most part between them and sometimes with the neighbors who were fond of it and knew nothing about hunting. My brother knew nothing about the woods, or use of a gun, unless it was on a general parade, or in a muster field, and there was far my superior. He was naturally fond of tactics and made it his study, and always bore some military or civil commission, and frequently both.

CHAPTER XV.

"THE DAYS WHEN I WENT COURTING."

S TO MYSELF, I had but little aim: if things went on well for the present, it was all right; the future, I studied but little. Like the most of men, by mixing so often in company, I fell into many little courting scrapes, of which I could say many things, but it would be useless, amounting only to nonsense. I was by nature an admirer of the fair sex; indeed, I had almost a superstitious veneration for them, for I thought a handsome, neat looking female, almost incapable of doing wrong; and to this day I can not avoid feeling a kind veneration for a decent, modest looking female. There is, however, unfortunately, a class, that degrade themselves and fall beneath the dignity of their nature; that class I fortunately avoided, and never in my life associated with. That fact, I doubt not, will be disputed by those who know me; it is, nevertheless. strictly true. Marriage was fashionable, as I presume has always been the case, and I frequently offered myself a candidate, having some serious thoughts on the subject. I was not in possession of property sufficient to make it an object with any woman, and had nothing but my own personal qualifications to rely on; I was conscious that even these were far from first rate, and that I must be content to stand in my own grade; neither did I make property the object of my pursuit, though some differed widely with me in that opinion; I thought there ought to be some congeniality in the mode of thinking and acting, and a mutual agreement in sentiment on all subjects that might be connected with our interests through life. Entertaining these views I made several selections—being frequently in pursuit of more than one object at the same time. In order to make myself friends of the unrighteous Mammon, on one side, in case of failure on the other, and often with no other intention than amusement, I was often well received, and the probability of success seemed favorable, there appearing a willingness on both sides; but the subject would die away without any apparent cause on the part of either. Again, I often found myself rejected; as often as otherwise. by the very persons I cared the least about—so upon the whole, I had little to boast of or regret; to tell the truth, I was by no means overly anxious. At length, one summer, or rather fall, there was a considerable demand for tobacco hogsheads, and a man of my acquaintance took an idea of furnishing a number. He understood the business, and proposed that I should join in with him. I consented, and went to work, taking in another hand, and hiring a couple more to saw a quantity of timber. There was a large quantity of tobacco made, and we could easily sell all the hogsheads we could furnish. We worked hard, early and late, tasking ourselves, after our timber was gotten out, at two hogsheads each, per day, when the weather was good.

The man with whom I was at work, was somewhat advanced in years, and had several in family, some of whom were grown. He had married a widow, with four or five children; the old lady's first husband had been a tailor by trade, and she, having worked a good deal at the business, had become a very good tailoress, employing herself mostly in that way. When the weather was unfavorable for out door labor, I always employed myself in working for her, without making any account of it. By taking a little pains to please, I had become something of a favorite with both, and by singing music with the young ones frequently of nights, of which the whole family was very fond, I found myself quite agreeably situated. The man's mother was still living, an ancient lady that had raised a large and respectable family, mostly sons. The old lady had married a second husband, who also had a family; she had become a widow the second time; all of the children of both families had married, except the two youngest of both families, who were daughters. The old lady still retained her ancient home in South Carolina, about forty miles from the place where I then resided, keeping these two daughters with her. She still possessed a few slaves sufficient to support the three. Not long after I had set in with this man, the young sister came on a visit to her brother, with the design of spending some two or three months; there being several young people about the house, I found it no difficult task to become in some measure acquainted with the new comer, neither did I feel averse to cultivate her acquaintance.

I made it a point to accompany her to church every Sunday, and sometimes to the singing school and occasionally to some little dance that might take place in the neighborhood; the old lady perceiving a little growing intimacy between us, seemed inclined to encourage it. It is generally the case when a woman wishes to accomplish anything, that they carry their zeal too far and by so doing injure the cause. She was, I thought, rather anxious,—however, the thing went on until I began to think myself most confoundedly in love. At the same time there was another little girl in the neighborhood with whom I had formed some previous acquaintance—a sister of one of those singing masters, whom I have spoken of, by the name of Neel—and I could not help keeping an eye on her, although she stood a little more reserved. I could see her always at church or the singing school, but at the dancing schools or little country frolics she was seldom to be seen.

When I wished to see her I had to visit her at her own residence. I was not confident that I could succeed with her, although there was a good understanding between her connexion and myself. Neither did I feel any very strong doubts. She was a beautiful singer, a little reserved in her manner, inclined to be serious and neither so handsome, so gay, nor full of life as the other, still I felt a little leaning towards her that I could hardly account for. She was an orphan girl, and destitute of property and living with her sister, but a man's preferences among females are absolutely inexplicable, and so with a woman towards men, but it seems the business was wound up. Here was a fine girl, full of life, with a good appearance, some property, and backed by friends of respectability and no objections on either side. Indeed my own friends were urging me on, and there appeared to be a perfect willingness with both myself and her, and if there was any other feeling between us I am a stranger to it to this day, and except some little liking that I had for the other, which appeared to me to amount to nothing at the time. Miss Jane, for so she was called, had extended the time of her visit something beyond the time her mother had given her, and it became necessary that she should return. Her good old sister-in-law proposed that I should accompany her on her way; I very willingly agreed to the proposal. She had four brothers that I was well acquainted with, and two others with whom I was not so well acquainted. Her youngest brother lived a few miles from her mother, and thither we concluded to go. She had but one sister, and her mother and sister I had never seen. I knew the news was getting out among them and I thought it prudent not to visit the mother and sister until they were prepared for the interview. I spent two days and a night with her brother; after setting a time to return, I started for home. I let the time for returning, pass over designedly, to see if there would be any grumbling. I now started on, hardly knowing that I should return until I was a married man. When I arrived at her brother's, all appeared to be right; I met Miss Jane, accompanied by another young lady, a sister to her brother's wife. On my first interview, I found myself *blazed* on by an unexpected meteor which almost stupefied me; the shock was almost as sudden as St. Paul's conversion. In the person of Miss Susan I thought I beheld the greatest beauty I had ever seen, and began to wish that I had never seen Miss Jane or any other young lady. In my first paroxism, I had a notion to forswear every other woman upon earth, to throw myself on her mercy, and in case she rejected me, never have a word more to say to the sex. But objects, by being in sight, soon become familiar, so by being in company, three or four days, I concluded she was nothing more than a very handsome and quite agreeable woman.

Winter was coming on and the cotton picking frolics were commencing in the neighborhood. There was one to take place at a brother-in-law's, some five or six miles distant, on the second night after my arrival, to which they had been invited two or three days previous. They were all going and I was invited to accompany them; the brother and sister-in-law knew nothing of my being in the neighborhood—to them I was a perfect stranger, and it would be necessary to play a little deception. We started late in the evening, so that it might be dark, and the company should all be gathered before we got there. This brother that I was now with, was remarkably fond of singing and there was one song that I was in the habit of singing, a little singular in the mode in which it was to be sung. This song he was taken with and frequently insisted on me to sing. After we started, said he, "If you will join me we will have some good fun to-night. There will be no danger, for my brother-in-law is fond of a good joke. He is very fond of passing jokes, and if you can put a good one on him he will like you the better. There will be several fellows there to night who will be quite gay, and I want to lay their feathers a little, just to have a laugh, and will be responsible to my brother-in-law and sister. I will introduce you as a travelling preacher, and you must keep on the mask until after the cotton is all picked, and after supper, when they are about going home, then propose giving an exhortation and introduce it by singing that song." The plan laid, he named it to the women, and they all declared they would keep it a profound secret. Here was an error in me, for I always believed it wrong to jest with serious matters. We arrived at the place just after dark, and according to expectation the company were all gathered, the house was full and all in high glee, and some three or four young fellows cutting up some pretty high shines to divert the rest. So soon as we stepped in, my guide introduced me to the man of the house, saying, "Mr. Green, I bring you Mr. ——, a travelling preacher; I hope he will be received, and sister H., I hope it will not interrupt your cotton picking." In a moment a whisper passed round the company and all was in profound silence. The preacher was introduced to a seat near the fire; those who were noisy on our first entrance, retired to the back ground and were silent. Mr. Green and his lady took seats near me and entered into conversation, while all my company were seated near. I was reserved in talking, and although I had every muscle of my face under complete command, yet I was sometimes afraid to turn my eyes on my companions. There was an old superanuated maid about the house that seemed compelled from neccessity, to live wherever she could, but she seemed to think she had religion, and being of the same faith as she thought I was, stuck quite close to me, and asked more questions than all the rest; however, she was frequently called off to see about the arrangements for supper, as that seemed to be her province. These little calls relieved me very much and my companions being aware of my situation and feelings would ingenuously try to lead the discourse into some other channel, when it appeared to be bearing too close. Time passed on and I do not think I ever saw as much cotton picked in so short a time by the same number of hands.

Supper came on; I stepped up to the table with a good deal of solemnity, and gave the company a rather lengthy grace. As soon as supper was over, they began to collect their bonnets, hats, and cloaks, in a very silent manner, preparatory to going. I was standing by the fire with my friend Samuel, for that was my companion's name, carefully watching their movements. Mr. Green and his wife were about the middle of the room, paying some attention; all were in motion, just ready for starting, when I spoke, and told the people, that if they would be composed, I would trespass on their time a few minutes. All were soon seated, in silence. I then said: "We will sing a hymn;" and without hesitation commenced my song; by the time I was done, Mr. Green and three or four others, fell prostrate on the floor; Mrs. Green was struck speechless, and Mary —my religious old maid, with eyes like two full moons, was perfectly motionless. Mr. Green was soon up and had me by the hand; "Well," said he, "stranger, I have seen many men, but I never was so completely headed before; if you will stay with me a month it shall not cost you a cent, and then you may go and preach as much as you please." Hats, bonnets, and cloaks, were quickly laid aside, and the fiddle out of its case.— Poor Mary, after collecting her senses a little, stretched out both arms, and with a solemn groan, exclaimed; "My friends, we ought all to be careful what we are about to night, for this is no man that has come amongst us—it is the devil!" shaking her head, she continued, "It is surely the devil! come to visit us for our sins!" It was not long before I was made acquainted with Green and his wife, in my real character; however, the dancing went on, and did not cease until sunrise the next morning. I would here remark, that there was not a drop of spiritous liquors at the place; neither was it common on such occasions. I am well aware that people, at this day, think a frolic could not be carried on without liquor ; but this is all a mistake. It became necessary that I should pay a visit to my intended mother-in-law, who I had not yet seen. So I set out with that view, accompanied by Miss Jane, and her associate, Miss Susan. When we arrived I was introduced to the old lady by her daughter, and politely received. The old lady seemed to be perfectly acquainted with me, although she had never seen me before. I staid about three days and spent the time, principally in visiting among the family relations, in company with the two young ladies. In the meantime, Miss Jane gave me to understand that her mother had a wish that we should postpone our marriage a few weeks in order to make some preparations. I was well aware there would be no difficulty with the old lady, and determined not to bring her to an explanation until the final crisis, so I thought I would let the thing rest as it was. It was my intention at the time, faithfully to fulfil the contract, yet I wished to avoid committing myself too far. I was in a hurry—was my reason for not consulting the old lady. I had in the interval, been in company with a little girl near home, and there was some little leaning that I could not account for clearly, and as the matter was postponed, I for the first time began to think if I could get off on any honorable terms, I would do so, but not otherwise ; there began to be some appearance of a chance during my stay. I had paid some little attention to her associate, Miss Susan, and she consequently became jealous of her, as a competitor and a rival. However, it was without foundation on my part and as much so with the young lady, for it was a mere whim of the brain. A jealous disposition in a woman I believe to be a great enemy to sociability or happiness in a married state. She had hinted the thing two or three times, but I still thought it no more than a joke, and knew no better until after she had proposed a postponement of the marriage, which I found was done with a view of making some discovery. After some explanation she proposed for the affair to fall back, to its former position. After taking a view of the affair, I determined to occupy the ground on which she had inadvertently placed me. I told her as things were I had a notion to make a visit to my father before enthralling myself. I had not seen him in several years, and it would suit me better now than after marriage. It would require three or four weeks' time and by my return, all things would be ready. She began to suspect she had been guilty of some error, and offered some apology, so all passed off. There was preaching on the Georgia side of the river, on the way that I was to pass homeward, and herself, with five or six others, was going over. On parting with the old lady, I told her that I would call on her at no very distant period, and perhaps make some requirements of friendship. She replied that she expected she would always be ready to grant any favor in her power, and so I started once more for home. On our way to preaching, I discovered for the first time that the affair with Miss Susan was not the only one with which she had found fault. There was a young man in the neighborhood who frequented the house during my stay, who seemed to have for his object, Miss Anne, step-daughter to the old lady. He and myself became a little familiar; the news being out, he made free in some of our walks, to enquire about the probability of a marriage taking place between Miss Jane and myself. It was a rule entirely at war with my feelings to give any explanation to a stranger on such subjects. I told him it would be a very desirable thing with me, but thought she was a prize not so easily obtained; that I had made some proposition of the kind, but she appeared to be distant on the subject; I doubted being able to get her to decide in my favor. He told me that he had drawn a better confession from her; that judging from her own confession, she had already decided. I replied that I suspected that she was only sporting with his credulity, in order to amuse herself; that women were fond of amusing themselves at the expense of men, when they could palm an absurdity on them. The subject was dropped, and his satisfaction was not increased further.

It seems he had communicated the conversation, and she had taken umbrage at my mode of proceeding, alleging, that as she had fairly committed herself, that I should have made an open confession. Jones contended for the propriety of the position I had taken; upon the whole I thought she seemed naturally to be a little jealous minded. As respected Miss Susan, I thought her to be much the handsomest woman; I thought also, that any handsome woman was apt to be vain; at the same time, I thought her to be as clear of that foible as any very handsome woman I had ever known. Besides I thought Miss Jane herself fully as handsome a woman as I wished to be plagued with, and I thought if I had to fall into the hands of a jealous woman, I should prefer an ugly one. If she should become jealous and complain to her neighbors, which would be sure to be the case, she would receive less of their sympathy.— In the next place, I thought that I had no right to communicate every thing I knew to every enquiring fool that might wish to hear himself talk.

Before we got to the place of preaching, I told her that I still had an idea of visiting my father, and that the time of my return was indefinite; that I hoped when I saw her again, all would be right; that I should not stay for preaching, as I had some distance to ride; so we parted, apparently with good feelings. At the time, I still thought that I would return and consummate the marriage, not dreaming of any thing to the contrary. After I had gotten off by myself, I fell into a fit of musing on the subject, and found that I was likely to halt between two opinions. I rode on; late in the evening I arrived at the house of my good old landlady, her sister-in-law. I had been there but a short time, before the enquiry was made:—
" Where did you leave Jane?" " Where she wished to be; with

her mother ;" was the reply. " Why, dear me! I thought you would bring her back to see us." "I tried to do so, but was disappointed ; I fear Miss Jane has fallen into the hands of some of her old sweethearts and has determined to stay there." " Oh!" said she, " I know Jane better than that. I expect it is you that has met with some one else that has turned your head." " No, indeed! If I lose her I shall charge it altogether to you. If you had been as good a friend of mine as you pretended to be, you might have kept her here, and then, I might have had some chance—but as it is, I am afraid the jig is up ; that you and her laid your heads together, just to make a fool of me."— " Oh!" she replied ; " I do not know how any young woman can tell when you're in earnest, for I am sure I cannot ; there is no getting any thing out of you, for you never will explain." " There is no explanation needed ; for I am always in earnest," was my reply." There appeared to be some mystery in the matter, which the old lady could not comprehend ; it gave her some uneasiness, for the mind of woman is inquisitive, and they dislike to remain in the dark about any thing. I left her, alleging she would get some intelligence, when she should again see Miss Jane.

CHAPTER XVI.

VISIT TO MY FATHER—RETURN TO GEORGIA—MARRIAGE.

IN THE completion of our work, the making of tobacco hogsheads, I left the old man's house and went to my sister's, my place of retreat, when out of business. After a short stay I was prepared to visit my father, but before starting, I had several interviews with my little girl, of whom I have before spoken. The result was, that on my return, we would be married. One of my brother's-in-law having concluded to accompany me, we started on our journey. On arriving at my father's we found all well; several of my brothers and sisters, or rather half-brothers and sisters—for they were children of the second wife—though much younger than myself, had got married and had families. There was some rejoicing on my arrival, for I had been absent several years. They were all living in the same neighborhood and consequently to gratify them and myself too, I was obliged to stay sometime. Here I was guilty of a little error, for which I hardly deserve forgiveness, although it was productive of no harm, and a thing that probably happens frequently, yet it might seem a little ungenerous. I had on the road, communicated to my brother-in-law, my intention of marrying, when I returned to the country where my father lived which was thickly inhabited. Of course there was a number of invitations from the neighbors for me to visit them. Among others there was a near neighbor of my father's who had known me when quite young; I was urged to visit and spend some time with him, and concluded to do so. I had a step-brother about my own age, who had been raised with me and he was still single, living with my father. He was familiar about their house and agreed to accompany me there. When I went, there were several young people about the house —some three or four more than belonged to the family. The familiarity of my brother among them soon made me acquainted. At that time it was fashionable for young people when assembled together, to sing songs, and very often, to dance. We had not been long together before the singing was introduced and I felt no unwillingness to take my turn among the rest. It was common for the old people to encourage the practice, and to often join in the amusement. When we got there it was in the early part of the day, and towards night more than a dozen had gathered in, and most of the company staid all night and quite late the next day. Among others was a young woman belonging to the house, who attracted my attention; she was just grown up, and as I thought, handsome; I soon felt anxious to cultivate an acquaintance with her; she seemed on her part to have no great aversion, and soon became quite familiar. I was urged by the old people to repeat the visit, which suited my feelings. I did not stay many days before going back, taking my brother-in-law along to make the interviews more agreeable. All things went on well, and I found no difficulty in obtaining a private conference with the young lady. This encouraged me, and I soon went again, and by this time found myself once more confoundedly in love; but "pleasures are like poppies spread"—the time was at hand when I was to meet with a blast. It was almost impossible to keep anything a secret, more especially from women; I had not communicated anything to my father nor any of the family, neither did I intend doing so until about to take my final leave. But my brother-in-law, in conversation with my father and stepmother, "let the cat out of the wallet." The old lady, (my step-mother) had kept a strict watch over my proceedings, and on making inquiries of her son, and from some jokes that had passed between some of my sisters and myself, she had learned the game I was playing at, and in her religious zeal she could not stand it; she found means of leaking out the secret to the girl's mother. This soon put me down to the lowest note in the bass.

Not aware of what had happened, I again called, but very soon discovered that something was the matter, for I could not account for her conduct. I suppose she would scarcely have spoken to me, if she had not thought she would punish me by letting me know she was in possession of the secret. After making some inquiries, she frankly told me what she had heard and how she had got the news; it was but too true. I scorned to lie and found it necessary to extricate myself the best way I could—but how, I was at a loss to know. She alleged that my conduct towards her was ungenerous; I confessed the truth of the report—told her, that at the outset, I had only professed an attachment to her person and company; this was nothing more than the truth:—that on the subject of matrimony there had been but little said—that she had not committed herself by expressing any sentiment in my favor—that she "had plowed with my heifer and found out the riddle,"—that now, she had completely the advantage of me. I told her, that if I lived to return, I was under the promise of marriage—but that nothing was sure until it was accomplished—that it was possible I might be disappointed; if so, it would not be for the first time—that I had been unfortunate in that respect, for I had more than once thought myself as good as married and had still failed, and it might happen so again—that I thought in that respect the minds of women were changeable—that if they were almost ready to marry to-day, and a better chance offered they would be apt to accept it, and perhaps be perfectly right in so doing—that I never intended to fly the path myself, but allowed all liberties—that I was a candidate for matrimony, and had been for several years, and in case of failure this time, I had thought of returning to my native country and take a wife there if I could get one, and settle among my friends, and with these views I chose her as an object worthy of my attention. That I had intended to explain my motives before I left her—that she might think of the matter until I, in case of disappointment, should return, which would be in a short time. She at length admitted that I might have the pleasure of her company if I desired it, as long as I staid, on condition that the subject of marriage should be left aside. So we remained good friends for the remainder of the time that I staid.

This was in the fall of 1792. In the course of a few months she married, and I saw her no more until the fall of 1817. She had raised a large family, and her eldest child, which happened to be a daughter, was married to a brother of mine, that had lived to be a kind of old bachelor. In the evening, after this interview, I went to my father's, a little out of humor with my step-mother; while sitting at supper, in a serious manner, I addressed the old lady thus: "Well, old lady, I am afraid I shall have to become a little troublesome to you." "Ah! how so?" said she. "Why I have a thought of taking a wife home with me and shall have to put you to the trouble of giving a wedding dinner or supper, and boarding my wife a few days." "Oh," said she, "if I like her, I shall think it no hardship." "Well," said I, "it is Miss M——, a great friend of yours; I have been courting her ever since being here and was doubtful of getting her, but you rendered me a good piece of service which brought her to a conclusion at once; you raised a report, you and Mr. B., between you, that I was engaged to be married on my return home. I told her it was nothing but a scheme of yours to get me off that you might keep her for your own son, my friend James ; she believed it, and said she would match you for being so cunning ; she suspected for some time, that you did not pretend to think so much of her for nothing. So the story was of service to me, for I do not think she would have come to a conclusion so soon had it not been for that." I pretended to be serious on the subject, and kept the old lady in suspense for two or three days.

The time arrived for my return to Georgia. My father who had given me many moral lessons, gathered up several books on religious subjects, and presented them to me, for my acceptance, enjoining on me to read them with attention. I received them with a promise, that I would read and consider them, at the same time, caring little about it, for I had not imbibed the same notions on the subject of religion that he had, but did not show any signs of aversion to his advice. Moral honesty, indeed I believe to be necessary for every man, and essential to the well being of every community, and determined within myself always to associate with persons of good moral character, and respectability or have no associates at all. On parting, I acquainted my father with my intentions and took leave of all my friends, once more for Georgia. In a short time after my return, I made up my mind and set in with a man, of my acquaintance, by the name of Petigrew, to make a crop. Soon after setting in with him, I informed him of my intention of marrying. He encouraged me to proceed, telling me he would assist me to set up housekeeping ; he told me he would stop all hands a few days, and put up a cabin that would answer for the season, and further, as he was bound to furnish my board, he would supply whatever provisions might be necessary for me and my wife, until the crop was finished, without making any account of it. I concluded, however, not to make the cage until the bird was caught. I had little to expend by way of making preparation for a marriage feast; three very good horses, a few articles of clothing and a piece of land was the sum total of my effects, and I did not think it advisable to sell a horse to make what was called a wedding. Her brother-in-law, with whom she lived, was a poor man and had a family, and I had no wish to cast any burden upon him. The news had got out, and I knew several that expected to be invited, so after consulting the man with whom I lived, I determined to cut the matter short, without making any fuss about it. I took my horse, on Saturday evening, and rode over to the place where she lived; staid all night, and on Sunday morning proposed my plan. At first, it was objected to by the man and his wife, but after my urging the matter a little, and giving my reasons, it was assented to. On Sunday, I went off and taking a man with me, obtained my license, called at my brother's, and engaged him to meet me at the place, next evening. I then engaged a young man and young woman, and her brother-in-law engaged a couple in the neighborhood, all to attend on the occasion, and the next evening, we met the whole party including the household, and myself being ten, and on the evening of Monday, the 22d of March, 1793, I was married to Miss Neil.

On Wednesday morning, the 24th, I went to work to build me a shelter; with the assistance of what hands there were on the place where I lived, with five or six of the neighbors that aided me, by Saturday night I had a kind of cabin to go to, and on Sunday, I moved my wife, with what few articles of furniture she had, and they were not many. I soon found that when a man gets a wife, he stands in need of some other articles; in a short time I sold a horse to procure some cattle and additional furniture. Stock was then valuable; the range on the frontier being good, by keeping them therein, they were very little expense, except salt. Shortly after, I sold one of my tracts of land, taking a good share of the price in cattle. I now turned my attention to the keeping and raising of stock, so that

I frequently had beef cattle and milch cows for sale. Cows and calves generally brought a good price, for new settlers were constantly coming in, but beef seldom brought more than three or three and a half cents per pound; the business also suited my propensities. As soon as I had gathered my crop, I rented a small farm, lying immediately on the river, for two years; my own land lay outside of the settlement, and there was danger in living on it, the Indians still being hostile.—The land I rented, was good, and a young man, brother to my wife assisted me in cultivating it. There was an excellent fishery belonging to the place, where by keeping some traps in order, there was an abundance of fish caught, especially in the shad season. There were iron works, or rather a furnace, that had been erected about twelve miles from my place, which made my fishery a source of some profit. I remained here two years, my brother-in-law still staying with me; at the close thereof, I concluded to cultivate my own land, though the Indians were still somewhat troublesome. There was a fort situated about a mile distant from the place where I intended to settle, and into that I concluded to go, while I was making my improvements. Accordingly, on the 22d of March, I moved to the fort; most of the inhabitants had left and moved out to their farms, but no one family would venture to stay alone at night; they generally worked in companies in the day, and three or four of them would collect together in one place at night. There were four or five families still remaining in the fort, and three or four more that lived near, would go to their homes of a morning and return in the evening; there were spies kept out, though this precaution was sometimes neglected, when all things appeared to be still. The proprietor of the fort had a small farm of twelve or fifteen acres, which I rented; he having put up a mill near the fort without having any hands to labor for him and had to attend the mill himself. The Indians had stolen all the horses that were of value from the inhabitants—they could not keep a horse of any value, unless well secured in a stable.

I had taken two good horses with me and in order to keep them safe, made use of a house inside of the fort, for a stable; we kept up no sentinels at night, not being apprehensive of danger. I had a very severe dog that I had trained to the woods, and could put my horse or any other property in his charge and he would defend it to the last; he made no friendship in such cases with any man though he knew him ever so well. I have frequently killed deer that I was unable to lift on my horse; in such cases I had nothing to do only take out the entrails, give them to my dog, drag the deer to the root of a tree and give him charge of it, and leave him twenty-four hours, without returning and never, in one instance, have I failed to find all safe, without the least breach being made, and I have sometimes, to try him, sent my brother-in-law, who often hunted with me, ahead, the dog never failed to defend the deer, until I came up. At night, when I shut up my horses, I always fed my dog at the stable door, where he would stay during the night. It was thought by many that some unprincipled white men who were well acquainted with the country had some intercourse with the Indians and urged them on to steal horses. Indeed the suspicion was so strong that some few of them fell under the displeasure of Judge Lynch, and left the country, and some three or four came up missing and were no more heard of. I myself saw two whom the evidence was so strong against— for they were caught with plenty of property in their possession—that they were subjected to no further trial than a council of fifty or sixty men and suspended between heaven and earth, at a cross-roads, and a snug hole made in the ground for them to repose in, where I expect, they rest in quiet to this day, unless they may at times, wish to arrest the attention of some nightly traveller, when the moon shines. These things passed off without being noticed by the authorities. One moonlight night, all in the fort were in bed asleep, and no apprehension of danger, my dog gave the alarm and some one in the fort called out, "There was some one at the stable door." A brother-in-law of mine who slept in the same house, and myself both sprang out of bed and caught our guns, when we got out into the square, we saw some one ascending the steps at the corner, by the sentinel's box, but before we would shoot they passed over they pickets and descended outside. We had no apprehension of Indians, thinking an Indian would not attempt to climb over, but supposed it to be some white man, and we would catch him with dogs,—there were several in the fort,—we immediately opened one of the gates, let out the dogs, and in our shirts, with our guns in our hands commenced pursuit; the dogs quickly took the trail and at a short distance, under some large poplar trees, by the side of a cow-pen, where a number of cattle were penned, they began to bay very fiercely; we advanced encouraging the dogs; when we had got within less than fifty yards of the place, thinking we had the fellow safe, our progress was quickly arrested by the report of four guns fired at us in quick succession from the shade of the poplars; we retreated with all speed into the fort and shut the gate, and then running up into the block house, discharged our guns towards the place, as near as we could guess. By this time all the men in the fort were under arms and at their places, expecting an attack. We called off the dogs and let them into the fort, and kept a good look-out until morning, but were not disturbed. Early in the morning, the alarm was spread through the neighborhood, and before night, the people were all in the fort. In the early part of the day, we received an express from another fort, about eight miles distant informing us that a party of Indians—whom we supposed to be the same who made their appearance during the night—had stolen fourteen horses, and that they had not finished collecting the horses until after day-break in the morning, and were discovered by a man that had been up and out in the fort early. They were pursued, overtaken, and all the horses recovered, but only one Indian caught or hurt.

CHAPTER XVII.

BOY ATTACKED BY THE INDIANS—FIRST SIN OF DRUNKENNESS—SPELL OF FEVER.

THERE WAS another fort not more than two miles distant from the one in which I lived. A river was between, and the people had to cross to the fort to get meal. A young lad had come over to the mill; he was well mounted and had a large bag of corn on his horse; after having his corn ground he started home and when about half a mile from the mill, in the river swamp, was met by a party of Indians; they were close on him before he saw them, and advancing on him, in plain English, ordered him to stop. It seemed, from their movements that they did not wish to kill the lad, but intended to make him a prisoner, and to take the horse. The lad was active and a good rider; he made a shift and on the first motion overbalanced the bag and letting it drop, put his horse to full speed. The Indians immediately fired upon and pursued him, and just as he ascended the other side of the river fired again, but without effect. We heard the report of the guns but could not account for the cause, supposing it to be at the other fort; however, we were soon relieved by the appearance of some men from the other fort. The Indians had emptied the bag and disappeared with it; the circumstance of their being discovered, in all probability, had prevented them from attacking our fort. This caused an alarm and the people were all cooped up again in the fort; the panic did not last long, however, for in a few days they all returned to their homes. This often reminded me of the speech of an old friendly Indian. He said—"White people were like hogs, when the wolf got among them they would rally and fight but as soon as the wolf was gone, they would all scatter and go to rooting." After this, the Indians did us little more harm, except stealing a few horses once in a while, which practice they continued for a year or two.

I forgot to mention in its proper place that when I had been married almost three years, in the winter before I moved to the fort, I committed my first sin of drunkenness. I will mention the circumstances which led to it, in order to show how far a man may be led astray without any intention, by falling into bad company. Some few days previous I had exchanged horses with a man, and he was to give me a cow and calf to boot. We lived five or six miles apart; one evening, I concluded to go over and stay all night with him and drive home my cow in the morning. I did so; the man told me the cow he designed for me was at a neighbor's house, where he had purchased her and had not removed her; the same night, another man with whom I was acquainted, came in to stay all night. The man, where the cow was, kept liquor to sell; in the morning, the other man that stayed all night, proposed to me, that if I would treat, he would go and help me drive my cow home, as he was going close by anyhow; I had no objection. I knew him to be a real toper, and that he drank hard; I was fond of liquor myself, and had been always accustomed to using it, but had never felt its intoxicating influence. I had been taught to believe that drunkenness was degrading, especially to a young man; I had seen many men drunk, and seen the evil consequence, and thought I never would be guilty; would to God I had always kept the resolution! But I am too late making the petition. I agreed to his proposition, and off we went; I came to the place, the cow was there ready, I called for a half pint of whiskey, I knew nothing about drinking grog. The whiskey was set out in a small decanter, containing the quantity called for, we soon drank it off; I prposed starting. "No," said he, "we must have another half-pint;" he called for it and it was not long till that was drank also, we then got our horses and I turned out my cow ready for a start. "Well," said he *"let's have a stirrup dram* and we will be off." I called for it, while on our horses at the door, "Now," said he with an oath! "if you don't drink your share we will thumb it this time," that is place your thumb against the bottle and drink the depth of your thumb, I complied and we soon drank that also. The day was cold and some light snow falling, however, we started. The cow was troublesome and the woods rough. When we had got about a mile she took advantage of the rough woods and running around the farm got back. I concluded then I would put a clog on her, we let her in the lot, caught her, and put on the clog. "Well," said he "we must take *another drink* and try the drive again." I knew that I had enough and objected, but he insisted and I hated to back out, so we went in and I called for another half pint. "Well," said he, "you must thumb it again, otherwise; you won't drink your share, so let us be in a hurry." I did not altogether relish the proposition, but had plenty in me to urge me on, and willing to be in a hurry thought I would risk it; it was not long before we despatched the other half pint. Says I, "Let's go." "Oh, no," said he, "we can take one more, and then go on to your house without suffering from the cold." He called for it, and commenced on it; I had reduced it one thumb, and sat down in a chair, when all of a sudden everything began to turn round, and the first thing I knew, myself, chair and all were down in the floor. I was perfectly sensible of all around me, and strove, in vain to rise; I could not stand. The man of the house happened to step in just then, said, "Hey, hey! what's the matter here? Collins down kicking? Well, it's a pity; for I expect it is the first time he was ever drunk in his life, and I will take care of him; he shall not suffer." Although drunk, I felt ridiculous, and must have had that appearance. However, the man got me up, put me to bed, and covered me up; I soon fell asleep. This all happened in the early part of the day, and when dinner came on, I was waked up; my companion had moved, decamped, was off. The family insisted on my eating dinner, but I was too sick—took a drink of buttermilk, and went to bed again and would have been gladly out of sight of every one; I was almost ashamed of my existence. When evening came on, several men of my acquaintance came in to take a drink; wishing to be concealed, I covered myself over, but after they commenced drinking, was soon discovered. "Hey," said one, "who is this you have covered up here?" "Oh," said the man, "it is Collins, poor fellow; he is a little sick." "What? Collins is not drunk?" "I believe he drank a little too much this cold day, and it has made him sick." All expressed their wonder, saying, "it was a new thing;" but to my mortification, I was compelled to get out of bed and set awhile with them; they insisted upon my drinking again to cure myself but I had no faith in the doctrine, and refused to comply. I staid all night, feeling sick and ashamed. The man of the house insisted that I should drink some, and recommended it as a cure, but the very idea was disgusting. I drove home my cow under feelings of sore repentance. I then renounced the use of whiskey and its charms forever; I determined it should never have any more influence over me; I would devote myself to the use of cold water, during life; a resolution that I would earnestly recommend to every young man, to make and keep, if possible. Experience induces me to recommend it, and I think, Solomon says, "Experience teaches wisdom." I kept my resolution for two years and six months, when, I was tempted to taste a little peach brandy; it seemed palatable, and I drank it on some occasions, but very moderately, for something better than one year longer, still rejecting whiskey. At length, we met on friendly terms; I found her to be an intriguing hussy and ventured once more to taste her, and there has, at times, been a great intimacy between us, especially of late years; the better the acquaintance the stronger the attachment, and I have often sorely repented that the acquaintance was ever revived after our first separation, and if I could have any influence over mankind, I would advise them to avoid any thing of the kind, not but that I believe the moderate use of liquor may be of benefit at times, but it is a growing evil, and hard to conquer, and if I had obeyed the dictates of my own reason, I should have quit it long ago.

But to return to the fort. My crop of corn was nearly ready to lay by, and I had made nothing else but a little flax. In the latter part of June, I took the first hard spell of fever, I ever had in my life; true, the measles, small-pox and fever and ague had all fallen to my lot, but a hard attack of billious fever I had never experienced; more than likely it was my own rash conduct that brought it on; while engaged one very warm day in saving my flax, near three o'clock in the afternoon, there appeared a dark, threatening thunder cloud; I worked hard and got my flax all safe; while suffering with thirst and foaming with sweat I went to an excellent spring near the fort, and without hesitation, drew up my pantaloons and waded into the stream just below the spring, and washed my legs and feet, not even taking the precaution of wetting my head; I then washed my face and arms—still standing in the cold water—until I felt quite cool and pleasant; I then went in and eat dinner and felt no harm; in the course of about an hour, I began to feel a dull pain in the head, and flushes of heat ran over me; I still did not apprehend any serious harm, but got my horse and gun and concluded to drive up some cattle belonging to the fort. I went but a short distance till I came across some deer. I killed one and it being in hearing of the cow bell, I went and drove them up. By the time I got to the fort, I was not able to go after the deer, but told one of the men where to find it, and he went and brought it. Before night I was completely out of my senses and continued so for several days; there was no doctor to be had except a Dutch quack, who used simples altogether; they brought him to see me, and I suppose he and the people in the fort did their best for me; I had never taken any strong medicine—there was no such thing in the country, nor any one who knew how to administer it, had it been at hand; I was perfectly insensible to every thing that passed; in this situation I had lain, for fourteen days, when at length they procured some flies as a last remedy, and applied seven blisters to me; I was remarkably hairy, and they made the plasters with paste in order to make them stick, and without the precaution of shaving had put them on; in removing the plasters, they had to cut the hair with the scissors; I still remained insensible of anything that was done, and they were nearly done removing the plasters when suddenly as if awakening out of a dream, I felt they were hurting me and complained. When I awoke, as it were, I discovered that I had not strength to raise my head off the pillow and was at a loss to know what the matter was. I saw the house crowded with people, all gazing upon me with great attention. I was reduced to a mere skeleton and no power to turn or raise my head, and knew not that I had been sick, and was entirely at a loss to account for my situation; some of them began to talk to me, and enquire about my feelings, but no one hinted their apprehensions, as I afterwards learned they had for several days, hourly expected me to die; indeed after viewing the situation I was in, I concluded that it was impossible for me to live, and it is doubtful whether, when the time does come, I shall be any better reconciled to my fate. But God had reserved me for further scenes for I am strongly inclined to believe that the way of man is marked out by infinite wisdom, and that he cannot turn to the right, or to the left without God; but is obliged to travel to the end of his journey, as it is marked out. I am well aware that it is a doctrine that many people do not believe, and that they would pronounce me a fool or a bigot. My old Dutch quack still staid with me; I asked for water, and he would not let me have any, for it appeared that all this time I had been prohibited from drinking cold water, and had nothing but warm teas or gruel to drink, and had eaten nothing. I continued in this way three or four days longer; the fever had left me, but still I longed for water, and could not obtain it, for I was altogether unable to help myself; I continued to swallow what medicines were offered me which was nothing but some kind of drops; at length I refused to take any more medicines, and told them I must have some water. The truth is, I did not expect to live, and thought I might as well be gratified in my last hours. The doctor flew into a rage and said he would leave, and that I would certainly die. Accordingly he went off in a bad humor, pronouncing me a dead man. A brother-in-law of mine, who was living in the fort, always insisted on letting me have some water; he contrived to get a bottle of spirits and kept it concealed, and every day, three or four times he would contrive to get all out of the house, even my wife among the rest, and would give me about two spoonfuls of very weak grog. It seemed to revive me, and I absolutely thought it the best thing that I ever tasted; this he kept a secret for several days, and to the astonishment of all I began to mend; though much reduced, my voice never failed; it was often remarked that when at the lowest they could hear me speak all over the fort. I was confined, in all, about ten weeks before I was able to walk across the fort. Although apparently well and hearty, yet my constitution was so impaired that I never got fairly over it to this day, for I have never had the same strength and action.

CHAPTER XVIII.

RETURN TO BUSINESS—DEATH OF MY WIFE—SECOND MARRIAGE.

HAVING recovered, I set about building, and improving my land; however, I also commenced work at the tailoring business, and by that means could make enough to hire two, and sometimes three hands to work on my place. I got a cabin put up, and some land cleared, during the winter, and on the 22d of March, moved to the place and then thought I was settled for life. I busied myself in selecting and planting some of the best fruit trees I could get. In the preceding winter people had moved out and were settling the country rapidly; it so happened that the country around where I lived was settled by that class of people who are called Presbyterians; they came to a conclusion to build a church and get a preacher among them; they accordingly set about building the church and made application to the Synod, and soon had a preacher sent on, and I have always had reason to believe him a good man. In arranging the different departments of church government, I was solicited to conduct the psalmody or music of the church, and besides was nominated as one of the elders. It was true I had thrown in my share for building the church, and was also subscribing for the support of the preacher, and had no objection to taking part in the music, but when it came to the eldership, I could not stand the pull—I could not subscribe to all the articles of their creed, and some of their ceremonials I thought altogether useless, and to act a part I did not believe to be right, would be gross hypocrisy, and so the office was declined. There was a considerable number of young people belonging to the congregation, and I taught a singing school in the church. I taught every Saturday, and as we only had half the time of the preacher, we met every other Sunday at an early hour, and sung until the hour of preaching; on these occasions, a number of married men and women attended and by this means, almost the whole of the society became good singers, and were able to carry all the parts of music in the church. I have often thought there was nothing more beautiful in church than good singing. In the mean time I had joined in with two of the most celebrated singers in the country, one by the name of Patterson, and the other by the name of Neblack; they were both young, or rather single men and employed themselves almost altogether in teaching music through the country. We selected a number of tunes from different authors, and called them Patterson's Selection. We made up funds to defray the expenses of printing, and Patterson went on to Philadelphia to superintend the printing and bring on a sufficient number of books to enable us to supply all our schools with the same kind at fifty cents per book. I continued the business nearly four years, by which means I realized about one hundred and fifty dollars a year. I kept a small farm and still attended to my stock, for the range was still good in the immediate neighborhood. At this period I was placed in a happy situation—was perfectly at peace with all men, for I lived among friendly, peaceable people, and if I had an enemy on the earth I did not know it. As to property, I had none to boast of, but I had as much as I craved; I owed no man anything, and if I had a use for a little money, I had it without applying to any man, and had a few dollars to spare my friends in case of need. There was one fortunate circumstance that attended me; my wife had no children, and I was not encumbered with a growing family; however, not many men would agree with me on the subject of its being fortunate; it is nevertheless true. I had no particular desire to be plagued with children, until they could run about and talk, and then they became favorites, and as things turned out, I have often since considered it a fortunate circumstance.

When I reflect, alas, where have all these happy scenes fled? They have vanished like the morning dew, and have become exactly the reverse—are only known by their dim shadows as I stroll about the haunts of old memories. I have often heard people commenting upon their misfortunes, losses, and disappointments, and thought it mere human weakness,—which perhaps was correct,—but, that I would never thus act; I have long since, by experience, found myself subject to the same error, still I ought rather to be thankful to that divine and mysterious power that led me safe through all the shifting scenes of life to the present time.

I had lived on my place near three years; there was then a great stir among the people about moving to what was then called the Western country : viz., Tennessee, Kentucky, Ohio and Indiana. A number of my friends and relations, assembled together with myself, after holding a consultation, concluded to form a company and all settle near one place, and to that end I sold all my land and stock and purchased a small negro, and got all things ready for a move. As above stated, we agreed to go in a company, as it was not safe for any one family to go across such a large scope of Indian country. Before the arrangements could be made, spring came on, and we concluded to put off the movement until fall. This caused me to labor under some disadvantages. I had more horses than I had present use for, and was obliged to be at some expense to keep them up; I rented part of a farm, in order to make corn to fatten my horses in the fall. I gave up my place, and on the 22d day of March, moved off and left it, having staid three years to a day. All this time I had continued to keep up my singing school. When fall came and the preparations were completed for the company to move, my wife was taken sick and was unable to travel, and after waiting a few weeks and seeing no sign of her recovery, they went on and left me. I employed three or four of the most eminent physicians in the country to attend on her: viz., Gilmore & Holt, of Eberton, and Philipps of Lexington, but all in vain; her illness increased and after lingering about five months, the scene closed in death, on the 27th day of January, 1801.

After the death of my wife, I disposed of what little furniture I had in my house in rather a careless manner, without deriving that benefit which I ought to have had; at that time I had not the most distant idea of ever attempting to keep house, or again wanting any furniture. I thought of leaving the country and pushing my fortune somewhere else; I had no incumbrance and thought it would then be easy to go to any place I might wish, having no particular place in view.

I had an idea then, in which I afterwards found I was entirely mistaken. I had heard in my youth, a great many remarks made among females about widowers, from which I concluded that men of that class had to stand in the back-ground, and this made me determine never to become a candidate for any place unless fairly eligible. I had on hand, several horses, and no use for more than one, and horses were not then ready sale for money; in order to get clear of some of my horses, I bought a four hundred dollar horse, and paid for it mostly in horse-flesh; by this means, I got clear of three of my horses for one. I kept that horse four years and sold him for the same price I paid for him. I next got clear of the balance of my horses on the best terms possible. In the course of a few months I resumed the business of teaching music again; teaching singing then was very popular, and those two men of whom I have spoken, Neblack and Patterson, both being single men, were engaged in the business pretty extensively. I joined in with them and we formed a kind of circuit; we attended the different schools, one after another, in our turns; I had, for the most part, to attend to the schools three days in each week, and so with the others; this business I attended to for something more than a year. In order to keep myself employed and also to make something, I engaged in another business. There was a Dutch potter living in the neighborhood who followed the business of making what was called crockery-ware. The neighbors around had got mostly furnished, so that it was not of very ready sale, close around him; he agreed, by my taking a quantity, to supply me at a reduced price, and I took it to a convenient distance where I could make sale; by this means, I was making a small profit. I was extremely cautious in trying to initiate myself into female society; indeed I never had the same slight, or the same assurance which I thought some men possessed in that respect, although, I believe I respect the sex as much as most men; I never was very intrusive. At length, when I began to venture, I soon found some of my ideas were incorrect, and that there was more owing to circumstances than to any real antipathy they had to the name of widower,—perhaps the circumstances of a young lady becoming a step-mother, might sometimes place her in an awkward situation, and be a good objection to her venturing. On my part there was no difficulty of the kind in the way; I met with no trouble or difficulty about any house that I frequented or among any people with whom I associated, yet I did not feel as though I was occupying my right place; I had been accustomed to having the control of a house, but now I did not feel myself at liberty, but was compelled to submit to the control of others, feelings that never had affected me previous to my first marriage. I was for some time halting between two opinions, and not able to decide, sometimes inclined to leave that part of the country and settle myself down in some way and become stationary; at times I was employed in reading the Bible a good deal—a book by the way, that I had often read, in my life. I also consulted the opinion of several writers on the subject of religion. I sometimes thought of dropping every thing else, and turning my attention to the study of divinity; on this subject I had several conferences with our clergyman, Mr. Newton, a man who I have always thought to be a pious christian. This preacher encouraged me to pursue the design, promising to render me every assistance in his power. I spent some time in consulting and comparing the creeds of different denominations and found upon the whole, that I could not in every particular agree with either party, but must differ in some respects from the whole, and under these views, to join in with any particular sect would subject me to act the hypocrite, and I thought hypocrisy the last thing a man ought to resort to, at least in religious matters, and to become a schismatic in the church, or stand alone as a reformer, required a man of greater powers of persuasion and criticism than fell to my share, and to avoid exposing myself to the public in attempting a thing for which I was not fit. I gave up the idea, and concluded to fall upon some other plan; I had in this time almost decided that I would marry again, if I could, on fair principles, and had been rather trying to make some selections. One day in the summer of 1802, when I was at one of my out-posts, or repositories of crockery-ware, I was sitting in the gallery with a book in my hand; I saw two women come riding up; I rose, went to the gate, and conducted the two ladies in; one was a married lady whom I had known for several years, the other appeared to be a young lady whom I never saw; I knew the married lady to be fond of a joke and after a short conversation,—" Well," said I, " Mrs. R., you have not been polite enough to make me acquainted with your companion; being a widower, you know and rather on the lookout for a wife, I don't like to be neglected by my friends." "I really beg pardon, sir, but it is not too late; this, sir, is Miss Anderson. Miss Anderson, Mr. Collins." I saw the young lady would gladly have avoided the introduction, especially the manner in which it was conducted. The old lady of the house who had known me for several years, and with whom I happened to be a great favorite, joined in with Mrs. R——, and they were not sparing on their young friend, Miss Anderson, with their jokes. I saw her cringe several times, as if she would willingly shrink from the subject, but it would seem like women have no mercy on each other, when they take a notion. After some interval, Mrs. R——, as if determined to torture the feelings of her young companion, again commenced. "Well," said she, "Mr. Collins, I want to get some of your crockery-ware, and have thought of a plan by which I can pay you very easily, unless it be indeed the trouble of telling a few lies. The proposition is this—I will get Mrs. P——, here to join me; we will throw our influence together in your favor with this young lady; between us, we can do something capital; you shall be bound to do your part, and if you succeed you shall not charge me for the crockery-ware—if you fail I am bound to pay you." I told her I would certainly do my duty, as far as permission went; that all I wished of them was to extend their friendship as far as they could, without committing their own consciences; if I was fortunate, all the ware I had was at their service, and more if required, but in case of failure, they should be chargeable with all the trouble that I was at in making the fruitless attempt. The terms were assented to by all but the third party, who was altogether silent, and no doubt glad when it stopped; however, Mrs. R——, picked out her ware and paid me for it without waiting for the result. The thing passed off and the two women departed. After they were gone, "Well," said I to Mrs. P——, "how do you like my wife?" "Your wife?" says she. "Yes, madam, are you not aware that was my wife with Mrs.

R——?" "No indeed," said she, "but wife or not, I think very highly of her, and do not think you could get a better one." After awhile Mr. P—— came in who had been absent. "Well," said I to him, "Mr. P——, my wife has been here to see me to-day, I wish you had been here to see us meet." "Your wife indeed! I should liked to have seen her very much, for I would like to know what kind of a looking person she is." "Well, I will describe her; perhaps you may see her some of these days and then you can tell me how you like her; if you should see a young woman a little inclined to be dark skinned, with very black hair and a speck on one of her front teeth, mark well—that is her." "Oh, well, if that is the description," said he, "I think I saw her not long since, but are you sure that she is your wife?" "Undoubtedly sir, I always knew my wife had to come to me, without me being at the trouble of hunting her up." "Ah!" said he, "that is a girl who has a little age and experience on her side; she is none of your young flirts and not easily trapped." I told him I had no notion to intermarry among children; I thought it a bad plan and all the chance was to marry an old girl or a widow. "Well," said Mr. P——, "if you make an attempt you will meet with some difficulties; in the first place her father is a very crabbed old fellow; he will not suffer every one to keep company with his daughter and if he is opposed to you, you will stand a bad chance; next, I know more than one, who wants that girl, and you will meet with opposition, and she is hard to please, herself; there is one of my workmen who is now trying; that is H——, and Mr. Tanottrer, and there is a namesake of yours; that would be three against you; however, I don't think you need dread but one, that is H——, and he is not deeply in the old man's good graces." "Oh," said the old lady, "you need not try to scare Mr. Collins, for I would almost warrant him success if he will try in earnest." "Ah," said I, "I shall be in no great hurry but will wait to see how the weather breaks- but she is certainly to be my wife ; that is a settled point." So the conversation broke off for the present, with a laugh, no one, I presume, thinking anything more of it than a joke, for I am sure I thought nothing else.

I saw the same young woman at church, once or twice, not long after, and from previous observations, took some notice of her. A few weeks after, she came back to the same place, in company with a married lady, the wife of a Baptist preacher. This time, as it happened, I had the chance of forming a slight acquaintance with her ; at the time, there were three or four mechanics at work at the place, and among them was Mr. H——, with whom I had been threatened as an opponent. I concluded to notice the movements of the parties to ascertain how they stood towards each other. I fancied there was a little anxiety on the part of the man, but if there was any in the woman, she had a better art of hiding it. After dinner, I determined to put his feelings a little to the test and take my observation. Being well acquainted with the head workman' but not so with Mr. H——, I went out to the work bench and commenced conversation. After some time thus spent, I said : " Mr. B——, what do you think of my wife on an average ?"— " Your wife? I am unable to decide, until made acquainted with her." " Are you not aware that is my wife in company with your sister-in-law ?" " No, indeed! neither do I know it now, only from your information ; however, if you say so, it is not for me to dispute it. But," he continued, " if you go to setting up such claims, you will get yourself into business, for Mr. H—— has already put in a claim." " Had I known this earlier," was my reply, " I would not have interfered ; but, having notified her of my intentions, it will not do for me to recede, or she will brand me with cowardice ; as my hand is to the plow, I cannot look back ; so Mr. H—— will have the hardest scuffle he ever had." I began to think of giving her a call and trying to form an acquaintance, but thought it not prudent to be in haste, and had a wish that chance, rather than design, should bring about a meeting; it was not long till it happened. There was a wedding to take place in the neighborhood, to which, a large number of people had been invited. The custom then was, for the guests to meet in the early part of the day, at the residence of the bride, the ceremony to take place about twelve o'clock, and the evening to be spent in amusement. My permanent residence at the time, was twelve or fourteen miles from the place, but I determined to be at the wedding. There was a man named Crow that lived close neighbor to my boarding place, with whom I was very familiar; he was a man that traded a good deal; he had business all through the country and knew every one. I had some business also, with several, that were invited; it was agreed between us, that we would go to the wedding, as if it were by accident, in order to save some riding. The day came and we went, allowing time for the company to gather before we got there. When we got in sight of the place, we saw some half dozen ladies walking along the road, meeting us; it happened to be the bride and her suite. After we had passed, I said to my companion: "Crow, what do you think of my wife?" "Was your wife in that company?" he replied. "Certainly; did you notice the one that walked with the bride?"— "Yes! do you call her your wife?" "I certainly do!" "How came you by that knowledge—did you ever ask her?" "I never did, but am aware of it by the cut of her eye, and it is my intention to put the question this day." He replied: "I will bet you a bottle of wine you don't speak to her on the subject; nay more, will stake the bottle that you don't say a word to her to-day on any subject." "Enough said! pay good attention, for I shall claim the wine."

We were well received by the old gentleman of the house, and spent the evening with the company. After the ceremony was over and during the amusements of the evening, I happened to obtain the desired interview. Crow and myself went home in the evening with Mr. P——, and stayed all night. The next morning I demanded of Crow my bottle of wine; in order to establish it, it was necessary to call on Mrs. P——, whose testimony in my favor was stronger than I believed it to be. For want of the wine being convenient, a dollar bowl of toddy for the company had to satisfy the demand. At this time, my mind on the subject of marrying was altogether undecided, although report had me married to some one or other every week or two. So fond are people of talking, that if a man and woman are seen talking together, whether they ever said a word on the subject or not, they certainly are going to marry. Some time after, I happened in passing, to call at the house where the wedding had been, and altogether unexpected to me, when I entered, behold! there sat Mrs. Anderson in company with the late bride. Before I left I had what might be called merely an off-hand conversation; I gave her to understand that I wished to visit her father's house; there seemed to be no objection; without any definite time, I told her that I should make free to do so. On such occasions I was always opposed to setting any particular time, and if I did was always sure to fail—designedly—and always sure to visit a day or two sooner or later; this I did to see whether they would fret or get angry at being disappointed, or accuse a fellow of telling lies designedly, and if they seemed to be too particular, I determined to quit at once. The father of Miss Anderson, I had seen a few times, but never at his own house; I had understood him to be a singular character, which I afterwards found to be a fact; her mother I had seen also, but was unacquainted with her; I had a slight acquaintance with one or two of her sisters, younger than herself, and she had a brother who had a family and lived close by her father, with whom I had formed some acquaintance. Ten or or twelve days had passed after I had seen her last, when I concluded to give her a call; to that end I mounted my horse and put off; I made it late in the evening when I rode up to the old gentleman's. He met me very politely, and invited me in; after conversing a short time, the old man spoke to his son, a lad, and told him to have my horse stripped and put away. I had looked around and could see nothing of the old lady, nor any of her daughters, only some of the younger ones, and objected to my horse being put away, saying I would ride over to Mr. P——'s. "Oh, no," said he "it is late; you must stay all night; my wife and daughters are gone to church and will be home directly. I am looking for them every minute; strip the horse Tommy, and have him put away."

I suspected from the old man's manner, that he was aware of my business; in a short time, the old lady and her daughters came home in company with two young men; one proved to be the man with whom Mrs. P—— had threatened me the first time that we were joking on the subject; the other man was paying his attention to one of the sisters, whom he afterwards married. Whether through feelings of politeness, or my being an entire stranger, no reason was there for me to complain of the reception that was given me. The sister and her partner seemed to interest themselves in my favor and take a pleasure in mortifying my rival's feelings. Never wishing to be tedious on such occasions, nor staying till people became tired, I started off pretty soon the next morning. I continued to visit the house occasionally for some time, until it seemed both our minds were made up to get married. At length, to wind up the affair, I called one evening to set a time, and consult with Miss Anderson. She expressed a wish to postpone the business. For some length of time I opposed the motion, and insisted on deciding at once; I told her to think of it until morning, and then decide; she professed to be of the same mind; I determined to use no persuasion, and took up an idea, which I afterwards found to be incorrect, but knew no better at the time. I thought she had a notion of playing the coquette, which in fact was measurably so but she did not think of carrying it so far, neither did she suspect that I would cut the matter so short. I told her I would drop the subject altogether, and the conversation stopped for breakfast. It would seem she thought I would take up the subject after breakfast and she would explain, but in that she was mistaken. Immediately after breakfast I took leave and departed ; I had been in the habit of calling at her brother's, which was but a few hundred yards off, and staying an hour or two. She concluded I would stop as usual, and walk over, and as it were, by accident, we would fall in company. However, this is her own statement, afterwards, and I have no reason to doubt it ; but when she got there, I was gone; she thought the match broken off. Mr. Crow, of whom I have before spoken, was making arrangements to remove to the State of Indiana and he seemed to be anxious that I should go with him. Several of my friends and relatives were gone there already, and I was somewhat inclined to go. I had but few arrangements to make, and could be ready at any time ; while Crow was arranging his business, I was dallying about, doing little or nothing. So things went on about three months with Miss Anderson, when one day, I happening in the neighborhood of her father, met with a young man, whom I have mentioned was courting her sister. He began to insist on me to call and see Miss Anderson ; I objected, and told him I never intended to name the subject again. He told me that I had taken a wrong idea ; that I was altogether mistaken ; that he knew how matters stood, and that if I called, no doubt but all matters would be set right ; I declined going with him at the time, but promised to meet him at the same place, on a certain day in the next week ; that I would think on the subject. I met him at the time and place, and went ; the subject was resumed and all things soon settled and we agreed to marry in order to avoid any further remarks, and on the 31st, or last day of March, 1803, we were married, I having lived a widower two years, two months and two days.

CHAPTER XIX.

HORSE PURCHASE.—A STRANGE DISEASE.

I BOUGHT a small farm in the neighborhood of where I lived before, and where I had once more settled, as I thought, for life, had once more married a poor girl, and was obliged to work. I saw the error of parting with what little furniture I formerly possessed, without remuneration. I now needed it and more too, and was obliged to pay a high price for every article required. Here I must relate a little anecdote, which, however trifling, has often amused me. I had but one horse and he was a very fine one; he was too fine to put in the plow; I had hired one for that work, until I could make a purchase. One morning I had been busy plowing, and came in to breakfast; my wife and I had just finished, when a man rode up to the gate leading a horse; he called—I went out to him and asked him to alight. "No," said he, "I'm in a hurry; is this where Mr. Collins lives?" "My name is Collins, sir." "Well sir, I was told at the place where I stopped last night, that you wanted to purchase a horse, and have called to see if I could sell you one." I told him I wanted one, if the horse and price suited me. He then began praising his horse and his good qualities. I looked at the horse and thought he might do a summer's work; he was old, but stout and strong looking. "Well, how much do you ask for your horse?" He replied, "I have always asked one hundred and twenty dollars, but am now willing to take a little less." "Your horse don't suit me sir; alight, perhaps you have not been to breakfast." "Well," said he, "I want some water very bad and will get down for a few minutes."— We went in, and I told my wife the gentleman wanted some breakfast. There was a negro girl about the house; my wife gave some orders about breakfast, and he immediately broached the subject of religion; my wife was a member of the Baptist church and he seemed to be inclined to the Methodist order. I did not incline to either; my wife was also partial to any one who would talk on religious subjects. I was not so fond of it, thinking there was a great deal of deception used; the two soon got warmly engaged with their subject, but she found herself rather headed; he was by far her superior. When the breakfast came on the table, he said a grace as long as a Scotchman would over a haggis. After he had eaten, he commenced his conversation again, and was very lengthy, so much so, that I thought he had entirely forgotten that he had been in a hurry, wanting to be at my work. He continued for more than an hour; when he finished, he bid her a kindly farewell, telling her to hold fast to religion, and saying, "I have a fine horse I want to sell your husband, but believe I cannot persuade him." She said that I would take my own way as to that; he asked me to walk out and give him a few directions. I did so, and went more than a hundred yards, he walking and leading his two horses. I stopped to turn back; "Well," said he, "you had better take this horse; you shall have a bargain in him as I need a little money, and will wait with you for a part of the price if not convenient to pay all, or take it in goods at the store." To cut the matter short, I told him it was in vain to talk, for I would not give him more than one fourth of what he asked. After beating about a while, he agreed to take in cash, twenty-five dollars and eight in the store; I agreed to give it; we went back to the house, I paid him and took up my saddle to put it on my new horse to go to the store with him. "Oh!" said he, "take your fine horse out of the stable and ride him, and put that poor fellow up and feed him, for he is almost famished; the man with whom I staid last night had not one grain of corn to give my horses; they had to stand in a cow-pen all night without a mouthful to eat, and have not been fed since yesterday morning; feed him and he will be ready to go to the plow when you come back." I asked him where he stayed; he told me; I knew the man had no corn to feed horses and thought no more about it at the moment. I took his advice, saddled my other horse, put the new one up, fed him, and off we went. We had about two miles to ride to the store; on the way I began to compare his religion with the price of the horse, and his other conversation, and I began to conclude that I must be cheated some way in the horse, and that if religious, he would be proof against liquor; if a hypocrite, I could contrive to make him drunk.

When we got to the store, I told the store-keeper to let the gentlemen have what articles he wanted, to the amount of eight dollars; he began to call down some articles at cash prices. "Don't you make a difference between cash and credit?" "Not a cent," said the store-keeper, "with this man it is all the same." There was company about the store, and I called for a bowl of toddy. "Come," said I, "stranger, I dislike a dry bargain—suppose we take a drink together." "Why," said he, "I seldom drink anything, but I suppose I must drink with you, as we have been trading." He got his goods and wanted no coaxing to take the next drink, and after taking three or four more drinks, he laid out five of his dollars. I was not much then in the habit of drinking; after I had got him fairly in a good way, I left him. He never left the store till night and then he was so far gone that he went but a few hundred yards, and laid down by the road-side, and probably fell asleep, for he had gone off in the night and left all his goods lying at the place where they were picked up, next morning; he came back next day, inquring for his goods, but no one could give any account of how or where he had lost them, but they were all at the store safe, and he got them. I had never seen the man before, nor since, but, on inquiry found he was a class-leader in the church, and a great hand to exhort. He certainly was entitled to credit; they called him brother Hopkins. When I went home, I asked my wife, what she thought of the man? She replied, that if all men were as good as she thought he was, there would be a better religious condition in the world, and all men ought to follow his example. I told her, I thought I was cheated in the horse. No. said she, he was too good a man to cheat any man; I have been looking at the horse, and he is worth double the money, and you have cheated the poor man because he is religious; I am surprised at you; it seems like you are an enemy to religious people; you are always persecuting them. Well, said I, we will see. I put my horse into the plow and he was the laziest I have ever yet seen; no whip nor anything else, would urge him on. I next tried the saddle; it was all the same, whip nor spur, answered no purpose; I got tired of him, turned him out, and put in my hired horse again. I fed him for eight or ten days, and rode him to a muster and swapped him away, and by paying thirty more dollars I got a pretty respectable horse. He had got the horse the morning he came to my house, from the man where he staid all night.

I lived on, made my crop and just commenced building me a house in which, if life lasted, I had no doubt I would spend many days, and here commenced one of the most singular incidents of my life. In detailing this, I have no doubt but that the most of mankind would think me as insane as Noah perhaps was thought, while engaged in builing the ark. It may be supposed that this was not intended for the public, but it is a strange, yet a mysterious fact, as the sequel will show. I expect and I know I would be branded with superstition, insanity, enthusiasm, and no doubt be honored with the appellation of a hypochondriac and maniac, especially among the medical fraternity, although I believe them to be as liberal in most cases, as most men, yet when they come across anything they can't define to their own satifaction, they dislike it, and dislike to admit any solution they can't make themselves. I shall venture the outlines, at the same time, allowing every doctor to think as he pleases on the subject, admitting my position to have every appearance of a grand absurdity. I was once opposed to the belief, as much as any man living, of witchcraft.

Some time during the month of October, of that year, I was taken with some strange feelings, for which I could not account. I could ride, walk, eat my meals, had no fever, nor any particular symptoms of disease. Still I was in punishment, could get no refreshing sleep, or satisfactory rest in any position; to attempt to describe my feelings would be in vain. I sent for a celebrated Dr. Morton; he came, drew some blood, gave me some medicine with directions, pronounced my case not dangerous, saying he would call again; he did so, gave me more medicine and left me, stating that it was not worth while to call any more—there was no danger. I found no alteration; waited two months before I attempted to try another; then went to a Dutch doctor by the name of Clemens, and Dr. Wright. I was under their directions until the next May; having received no berefit from their treatment, I was advised to try an eminent physician, Dr. Shelton, of Pendleton District, South Carolina who, it was said, cured almost everything; numbers having gone to him for more than a hundred miles distant, and never failed to get relief. At this time my first child was born.

I got a carriage, took my wife and child, and started for Dr. Shelton's, intending to stay until I could get some relief, if possible. When within six miles of his residence, I was informed that he had died a few days previous. Upon enquiring, I was told that there was a Dr. Edward, about seven miles distant, who had studied and practised under Dr. Shelton, and it was thought he was as good. Concluding to go to him, I went and called on the Doctor; after some conversation, I told him my business; he examined me minutely respecting my feelings and what practice I had been under; he said that if I would remain with him three weeks he would cure me; that he would not undertake to board me, but would furnish a good room with a fire place; neighbors were plenty and I could procure any thing that was wanted, and as my wife was along, she could cook for me and herself. "If I fail to cure you," he continued, "you shall not pay me a cent, neither for the room nor my services; if I perform a cure, I shall charge you what will be moderate, and you shall have the liberty of my shop, and my books, if you wish to read; in a while I can learn you to mix up medicines, and have no doubt we shall be good company, so there will be a pair of us besides your child, for my wife has no children."

I took with the offer, and settled down for three weeks. I was under the immediate superintendence of the doctor during the time, and he paid every attention, yet there was no change effected. When the time had expired he told me he wished a confidential conversation with me, and we went into a private room, alone; he wanted to ask a few questions, and wished me to give a candid answer. He then asked me if I had ever heard of what was called African poison, or was called by some, tricking. I told him I had often heard of it, but was altogether an unbeliever. The idea was too absurd, to suppose, even if it could be done, that such a snare should be laid for me, or for any other individual alone, so as to affect others who were equally liable, and I doubted the possibility in any way. "Well," said he, "we medical men reject the doctrine as an absurdity, and indeed it is against our interest to admit it, and that there are few who believe it, but a man may be convinced against his own judgment. Dr. Shelton and myself have had three cases exactly the same as yours, and failed in all, and two of the men got perfectly cured very simply, by applying to an old African and are now both well and hearty men, and he performed the cure altogether by some art, I know not what, but without any kind of medicine, and that in a short time ; the other poor fellow never applied and finally died. I should dislike very much for it to be known, that I admitted the belief, but as sure as there is a God in Heaven it is what ails you, and unless you can get some remedy in that way, you will never get well. All the doctors and all the medicine in the United States will not do you any good and you will spend your money and time in vain ; I have had as fair a trial as I could wish ; your constitution is good, there are few such, and you are absolutely free from any kind of disease ; I am candid with you and feel myself interested in your recovery, and be assured, if you ever get well, you will find the truth of what I tell you."

I thought at the time it was a strange lesson for a man of science, and wondered how he could admit such absurdity. He stated that the negro who had performed the cure on these two men lived about ten miles distant, and in order to give me some proof of the correctness of the doctrine, proposed the following plan : viz., " I will write to the owner of the negro ; I know him to be much of a gentleman ; I will request him to let the negro come to me, not mentioning any business. The secret must rest between you and me ; will speak to my wife to go over and tell Willie Gibson, a young man who lives in sight, to come over-- I wish to see him—your wife can go with her. I will hire him to go after the negro, not letting him know anything, nor any one else, not even our wives. You and I will stay together, and speak to no one separately, until he comes. You are an entire stranger ; he nor no one else knows anything about you, in this vicinity, and if he tells you it is the case, or any particular circumstances or reason for it, then you can judge for yourself or draw your own conclusions.

He sent for the young man and wrote for the negro as proposed; he came in the dusk of the evening. I was lying on a bed, the doctor and the two women sitting in the same room; it was announced by the young man that the negro had come; the doctor asked him into the room; after some compliments had passed, he told him he had a sick man he wanted him to look at. "Well," said the black, "let's see him." He could not speak very plain English, but sufficiently so to be understood. Being requested to get up, I did so, and presented myself before the magician, the first that had ever undertaken to tell me of past and future events, relative to myself. After viewing me a short time, he began to consult his oracle, ephod, or whatever name you might choose to give it, for I have none. I asked no questions, neither did he; I felt a little sullen, thinking it would turn out to he mere balderdash. He began by telling of past events; in this he somewhat surprised me, for he told me a number of facts that it was impossible for any person but myself to know any thing about; not even my wife knew anything about them; at length he told what the doctor had predicted and what was the cause, and how it had been conducted. After he had done it, it was as plain as Daniel told Nebuchadnezzar's dream; he then performed some kind of spell or charm to prevent, as he said, any further progress of the complaint, and told me that if I would stay some ten or twelve days, he would cure me; that he could not do it in a shorter time unless he could go home with me, and in that case it would not take him over three hours. The negro had told me the truth as respected circumstances, which I could not account for, because I knew there was no possibility of his getting any communication on the subject, yet I was still an unbeliever,—I could not swallow the doctrine. If I had, I should have certainly staid the time. Next morning, after some more conversation with the doctor, I paid his bill and dismissed him; on the day following, I took my leave of the doctor and his amiable lady with feelings of the highest esteem and gratitude and steered my course for home. On my return, the natural inquiry was, "Has Collins got well?" "No, I believe not." "Oh, there's nothing ails him but the hypo; he will soon have it as bad as Edmund Beezly had it." Well, I could not contradict it; It might be the hypo, for I know not what the hypo is. I perhaps have had it more than a hundred times, and perhaps have it at the present moment, yet I know not what it is, nor have I ever met a man of science who could fairly solve the question to their own satisfaction, much less to mine, who makes no pretension to science. It is a certain something for which they can prescribe no specific, and for aught I know it may be what our Savior supposed to enter the swine, or perhaps Pharaoh and his hosts were possessed of when they pursued the Israelites into the Red sea, and I presume it would hardly be doubted that it was the evil spirit from the Lord that troubled Saul when David had to play before him on the harp. At all events, I may have been subject to it at times, all my life, for I am not like some people I have seen; it would never offend me to be accused because I could not tell whether it was true or false. I would always admit the possibility, because I knew of men of more sense than myself to preach the doctrine, and I think it a bad rule for a man to condemn the opinion of his superiors. But admitting I had the hypo all my life, I never had it in the same way before. There was a man by the name of Gilbert, who lived a close neighbor to me, and who had been in the same situation for about three years; he was wealthy and had money to spend, and he had applied to the best physicians; he had gone to Augusta and Charleston, and tried the most eminent of the faculty, at both places, without success, and had tried the Warm Springs, on *French board*, and obtained no relief and finally by the suggestion of some friend, applied to an old African and was perfectly cured, in a short time, without medicine and nothing more than what people called conjuration.

I knew all this, but like most of people who are inclined to join the strong party, forgetting a lesson that I had learned in my youth, that the weak party had gained their independence and freedom; but joined in the general hue and cry, hypo, hypo.

I had lived neighbor to Mr. Gilbert for more than four or five years, and spent a good part of my time, while a widower, about his house. I could then write as fair a hand as most men, though at this time, for want of eyesight and steady nerves, I find myself vastly deficient. I was a better calculator than Mr. Gilbert, although he was a man of business; he used to employ me to regulate his books, examine his invoices, and lay on his per centage; he professed a great partiality for me, and I never had any reason to doubt his sincerity. I used also to keep him in fresh beef in the season of shooting matches; he always furnished the money, but never failed to get beef by my shooting. This Mr. Gilbert frequently told me that I had better apply to this old African for relief, as he had done, for he thought my case exactly the same as his had been. I was still in doubt, being opposed to his doctrine, and suspecting, that if any thing of the kind had been done to me, he was concerned in it, if not the sole cause; besides, I did not like him. At length, I concluded to try him. He came and stayed some two or three days; I got some better. but did not like the negro or his master, thinking them both to be knaves. I thought if any such miracle could be wrought, that the master could do it, and that there was an understanding between them in order to make money, for the negro was always employed in such business, or engaged in cock-fighting. His master was an old bachelor and had no family, but a few blacks; he kept close to the gambling table, and followed horse racing and cock-fighting, always keeping old Harry, as he was called, with him, invariably betting on his judgement. My dislike to old Harry and his master, induced me to dismiss the old fellow and pay him up.

CHAPTER XX.

VISIT TO A CELEBRATED DOCTOR.—A NEW AND STRANGE RELIGIOUS SECT.

WAS THEN LIVING in Franklin County, Georgia. I sold my small farm, and moved into Jackson County, in the neighborhood of my wife's father; and there rented a small place and took an English school. For two years I continued in that business. I had an attack of fever in the fall season, and came very near dying. Still being subject to this hypo, in addition to the fever, on my recovery from the latter, but all was not right. I had a brother who came to see me from North Carolina. I concluded to make one more trial with a doctor. There was a celebrated Dr. Freeling that lived near Salisbury, North Carolina; he was noted for skill in his profession, and his fame had gone abroad in every direction; he had emigrated from Germany at the time of the revolutionary war, and settled in Carolina; he professed to judge complaints or diseases by their external appearance, and it was said that he could cure every thing in that way. I determined to make a trial, and went on in company with my brother, stopping at my father's a few days. The distance from home was some three hundred miles; on the night before we arrived at the Doctor's, we staid at the house of a widow lady named Duffy. The old lady, as old women generally are, was quite inquisitive, and finding that I was from Georgia, asked among other things, about Mr. Neblack, whom I have mentioned before; it seemed that she was his aunt and had heard nothing about him for two or three years; she seemed to be very glad to hear from him, and the account that I gave was somewhat flattering to the old lady; in consequence of my acquaintance with her nephew, she would have no pay. Next morning we started very early for the Doctor's, having about six miles to ride. I determined not to tell him the lamentable tale that I had the hypo, and had come near three hundred miles to get relief through him. I thought the better way would be to state that I was travelling on business through the country; that I was in bad health from some cause, and it not being much out of my way, I had called on him for some relief. When I arrived at his house, there was a considerable appearance of wealth; there was no alternative; I had to introduce myself, and my natural rusticity rather unqualified me for the approaching scene. I entered and asked to see the doctor. I was very agreeably relieved from any apprehensions, and was immediately met by the doctor, himself,—a plain, familiar, corpulent old Dutchman. He immediately ordered our horses to be taken care of, and well fed; we were then conducted into what I supposed to be the common hall; I determined not to be tedious—I told the doctor my motive for calling and at his request, furnished him with the outlines of my situation. I had thought from the character of the man that he could cross his fingers, turn his back to the moon, and pronounce a few Dutch sentences, and cure anything, and even drive the devil out if he had possession of the man. There were three or four young looking men, and all seemed busy reading. After the doctor had waited the time he thought proper, he asked me to walk into the shop again, and began to examine my situation, and made some remarks; he then observed to me that I had perhaps suffered considerable inconvenience from riding so much, he then filled a small bottle of some kind of tincture, took a piece of paper and wrote down directions how to use it and told me I would find it convenient in traveling; he then asked us up to the board to take a glass of peach brandy; by this time dinner appeared on the table; we set down and ate an excellent dinner. Some time after dinner I proposed taking leave, and asked the doctor his charge, and he dismissed me by my paying one dollar and fifty cents for all. I found the doctor to be a very plain old Dutchman, full of humor and anecdote; he told me he came to the United States as a surgeon with his Majesty's troops—that he was friendly to the American cause and that he found means of making his escape, and got among some of his own countrymen about the Moravian Town, and kept concealed until peace was made. He then married, settled, and betook himself to his profession, and his practice became extensive which made him wealthy. I left him and started back to my father's. "Well," said I, "I have made a grand speculation; I have rode more than three hundred miles, to see the celebrated Dr. Freeling and the interview cost me one dollar and fifty cents, and I am returning just as I came. This is grand indeed—this is certainly the hypo—and he even did not tell me that." We rode on that evening about twelve miles to a Col. Caldwell's, if I mistake not, on the south fork of the Yadkin, and for the sake of convenience, we had to stop a little before night, or run the risk of riding some time after dark. The gentleman of the house it seemed was not at home. In passing about I saw an uncommon number of black cats, and out of curiosity, asked the old lady, how many black cats she had? "Why," said she, "we have only nineteen at present. Mr. Caldwell took a great fancy to black cats, and concluded he would have twenty, and has often had the number, but somthing always happens to the twentieth, and he can never keep more than nineteen black ones at a time." This put me in mind of a similar circumstance that I had known in Georgia. There was an old Dutchman who lived close by my wife's father, who took the same notion and often got twenty, but could never keep more than nineteen; my wife will laugh to this day when she thinks of the old Dutchman's black cats.

I came to my father's, where I spent ten or twelve days.— There was then a great excitement about religion; there had sprung up a new sect, especially in the upper and northern part of North and South Carolina. I knew not what they were called, but they certainly were a curious sect; any man, no matter what he was, or where he came from, if he had impudence or self importance enough, was admitted to preach or exhort, among them. They had praying, singing, laughing, and dancing exercises; the jerks, the falling down, barking and laughing, and sometimes, the fighting exercise; the exercise of love, which was the best of all. During my stay at my father's, I attended two of their meetings. One Saturday evening, my brother told me, there was to be one of these meetings the next day, some distance off; he proposed to me to go and he would accompany me; I agreed, and early the next morning we set off for the place. When we arrived, the people were assembled; the house was crowded, all sitting in silence. I stepped in; I was a stranger; I stood on the floor for two or three minutes, seeing no vacant seat; at length, one man rose, and without speaking, handed me a chair. As I seated myself near the door, all eyes turned upon me, as if in expectation. I sat still; after some time had passed in silence, one got up and addressed the assembly in a few words; then prayed. A second and third followed, when all joined in singing; after singing some time, all dropped to their knees and commenced praying aloud, so that no man could tell what was uttered. After a considerable length of time spent in this way, one stout looking fellow sprung to his feet, clasping his hands, giving a tremendous stamp on the floor, and making a loud shout. All followed the example, and every man and woman began to exhort, or whatever it might be called, for it very much resembled the confusion of Babel, when the languages were confounded. When this had lasted some time, some began to fall prostrate on the floor, some began to dance, others to laugh, and some of the men and women to be very loving; others were stamping on the floor—striking their feet together and shouting. There was a large table in the house; a surly looking fellow got on his all fours and began to bark under it like a dog, once in a while jumping back. It seemed by some means the devil had slipped himself into the house unawares, but the fellow had struck his track, trailed him up and brought him to bay under the table, where he had attempted to conceal himself. In order to witness the scene, they crowded around the table, where they began to kick, and stamp, and hiss on their dog, and seemed to be determined to punish the old fellow for his intrusion, if they could ever get their dog to seize him. My situation began to be unpleasant; I thought I was in danger of being run over, and thought my neutrality would subject me to the suspicion of being rather friendly to old Nick, and that I might have to pay the forfeit in the same way, that he was likely to do. I thought it advisable to be off, and slipped myself out of the door and stood near a short time, and my brother and two or three of his associates, who were neutrals like myself, came out; we walked off a short distance, to where our horses were tied, and sat down; the uproar continued sometime, but how they disposed of the devil, I never learned. At length they began to pour out of the house like bees swarming, shouting and clapping their hands. This is a faint description of the fact. I attended another meeting of the same kind, only not quite so bad. After I had got to the place, one fellow got up, took a text and began to preach. After he had gone on some time the people began to be struck down, and considerable confusion ensued—shouting, singing, dancing, praying, etc. At length one fellow discovered the devil to be in the house and gave the alarm, and immediately attacked the old fellow for a fight, fist and scull—at it they went, and presently they both came on the floor. I could not see the devil indeed, but the other fellow appeared to be in a hard scuffle, down and up, over and over. The people crowded around, shouting and encouraging the fellow; at last an old lady who I supposed to be the wife of the fellow who was engaged in the combat, rushed forward slapping her hands, and crying out—"Well done, Johnny! Gouge him, Johnny! Bite him, Johnny!" At last a stout and brave looking fellow, perhaps more friendly to old Horney than the rest, but not willing to see a friend abused, he jumped up and smacking his hands together and stamping on the floor, roared out, "What, has the devil no friends here to-day? Hurrah devil! Gouge him, devil! Bite him, devil! Fair play, there shall no man touch! Hurrah, devil! I'll stand to your back." At length old Clooty, perhaps getting a little out of wind, got out of the house; the fellow with whom he had been engaged, pursued determined on revenge. All followed and the man who had been speaking left his stand, and clapping his hands and shouting, urged on the chase. All pursued, their hero in front; there was a large tree at no great distance from the house and it would seem that old Sam, to save his bacon, had to climb the tree. The fellow kept the track and presently began to bark up the tree. He made several attempts to climb, in pursuit, but it was so large he could not ascend, was obliged to content himself by barking at the root. They all gathered around, some throwing sticks to make him jump off, but in vain. Old Harry like a bear that had been sorely worried by the dogs, was feign to bear all their insults, and secure himself by sitting among the limbs and looking down, perhaps with contempt on their efforts. Fortunately for old Cloots, there was no axe convenient, else I think, they in a rage, would have felled the tree, and if so, his case must have been desperate. After wearying themselves in fruitless attempts to get the old fellow down, they retreated from the house and left the place.

CHAPTER XXI.

PREACHES A SERMON—MYSTERIOUS CURE.

DURING THE TIME I was getting ready to leave my father's, he had been busy selecting some books which he wished to present to me for my perusal. Among the number were Davis's Sermons, Harvey's Works, some of Calvin's writings, and some of Tillitson's, together with a small Bible. I could not refuse the books because they were from my father, and perhaps for the last time, which proved to be a fact, for I never saw him afterward. My father and brother both made some inquiry about my funds; I told them I had plenty, which in truth was not the case; but I was too proud to own my poverty. I took my leave and started for home. It was late in the morning when I started, and I travelled no great distance that day; I made it a rule in travelling to start early and ride ten or twelve miles before I stopped for breakfast, and then have my horse fed and stop no more until night. After I had gone some distance I began to consult my purse, and found it rather lighter than I expected; I began to repent almost of my pride in not accepting some relief from my father and brother, but it was too late. I had now to get along the best way I could ; I stopped for the night and started on, early next morning. Soon after I set out it began to rain. I began to apprehend I should be detained by high water, as there were a number of bold streams ahead, and in case I was much detained my money would be sure to fail, and I began to study what plan I should fall on ; from external appearance I knew it would be thought I had money plenty, and for a man to wear good clothes and be otherwise well fixed for travelling, to attempt to beg, he would be suspected of being an impostor or be liable to be insulted. At length I concluded to take advantage of the religious excitement at that time prevailing. I had once before traveled in company with a man and we both got into a similar situation ; our money was nearly expended, and he proposed that we should stop at the first convenient place and he would undertake to preach a sermon to raise a little money ; if I would act as clerk, that is, give out the hymns, and sing on my part, and he would perform the balance. I agreed, and we stopped near a church ; he proposed to the man where we stopped that if he would send out word to the people, that he would preach to them the next day. It was readily agreed on ; we were well entertained to the next day, when he preached sure enough. I performed my part without difficulty and we got money enough to go on our journey. I thought in the present case it would be no great harm to play the same game ; the greatest difficulty with me was—I was opposed to praying in public. Though my father used to enjoin it on me when I was under him—he was in the habit of keeping up worship in his house regularly, and he enjoined on his sons as they grew up, to perform that duty at times in his presence, being of Solomon's opinion. "Train up a child in the way he should go and when he gets old he will not depart from it ; " but in my case, Solomon and he, both missed the figure ; there was another rule that was practiced by the people in my raising—it was thought to be the duty of all mothers of families, in case of the absence of husbands to perform the duty of prayer in the family; it was enjoined by the clergy and a matter of censure if they were known to fail, and I in passing about, had frequently been called on to do that duty in place of the absent husband; although I did not like the business, I disliked to back out especially if there were any good looking girls about the house, which frequently happened, but to my story. I rode about twelve miles on the morning of the second day, when I stopped at the house of Mr. Cunningham, to get some breakfast and have my horse fed, and being after the usual hour, I had of course to wait awhile. I intended to let my horse rest an hour or two, and while I was waiting the rain increased so that I determined to stay until it would cease to rain so hard. I was very reserved in conversation; indeed I was so to a fault, especially among strangers. I seldom attempted to take the lead in conversation, preferring to listen to wiser men than myself, in place of much talking. Mr. Cunningham seemed to be fond of talking and in a short time, brought on the subject of religion; it seems he was a member of the church, and very zealous in the cause; he seemed to advocate the cause of the present revival, that had taken place; this seemed to me to favor my plan. I alleged that in some things I thought they had carried the matter a little too far, but perhaps it would be a bad plan to try to suppress it, for it would naturally cool after a while, and then the superfluous part would drop off. He predicted a great reformation to be in progress, and I did not hesitate to admit it; I soon learned enough to venture imposing on his credulity. I told him that I belonged to the clergy and preached when at home; that I had been called from home on important business and had been detained longer than I had expected, and that my funds were almost exhausted, and I disliked to beg; that if I could meet with a convenient chance, I would stop and preach a sermon in order to get a little help that I dislike to ask anything from people that perhaps cared nothing for religion. He seemed to rejoice that I had called on him, and told me he was confident he could be of service to me and it would give him a great deal of pleasure. He told me there was a place some miles ahead, perhaps eight or nine called Van Zandt's meeting-house, and people would be glad of preaching; that they had no preacher then living among them. "If you will consent to it you can stay with me and have a private room with a good fire place where you will not be interrupted. I will immediately send on a boy to one of the elders —have now forgotten his name; he lives about six miles from here and will write to Mr. Van Zandt, and will get the other to forward it to Mr. Van Zandt who lives close to the meeting-house and they will notify the people, and I will give you a letter of introduction to Mr. Van Zandt; I would like to accompany you myself, but I have some business that I am obliged to attend to, that I cannot put off." I told him to let the appointment be to-morrow precisely at twelve o'clock, for time was pressing with me, and would not admit of any delay that could be avoided. As soon as the boy was dispatched in the rain, I betook myself to the room as quick as convenient, and determined to keep myself as private as possible. I now had a hard task before me, upon which a good deal depended, and in which there was some risk. I therefore required some pretty serious study for the event. I had some doubt respecting my capability to perform the task before me, and set about preparing for it with all the energy I could command. I got out all my books and began to examine them, in order to find a subject on which to found my next day's work. I chose for my subject the twelfth verse of the seventh chapter of Matthew—"Therefore all things whatsoever ye would that men should do to you, do you even so to them; for this is the Law and the Prophets." After preparing some introductory remarks, I arranged the subject in the following order, to wit: In the illustration of the subject, I proposed: First—To offer a few things for the right understanding of the rule of social duty. Second—To consider the reason of it. Third—To open its excellency. Fourth—Mention important instances of particular cases to which it should be applied, and lastly show the necessity and advantages of observing it. I will remark here, that it might be doubted whether I could remember all these things correctly; if I had to rely on memory alone, it might be fairly doubted, but in all my travels, I was in the habit of keeping a daybook or kind of journal, and carefully noted down every particular, and I find myself yet in possession of a number of those papers to enable me to be correct. In the evening of the day, the rain ceased. Mr. Cunningham seemed to be a man of considerable wealth, and there was a store in sight, in which he seemed to be connected, and people seemed to be passing to and from the store during the day. In the evening I heard him from the window, of my room, tell those who were passing, that there was a strange preacher to preach at Van Zandt's Meeting-house, on to-morrow, and to give out the word—it seemed he lived out in that direction. On the day appointed he furnished me with a letter of introduction, as he had promised, and it would seem from circumstances, that he was a man of influence among the people. I left him and started on my journey, determined not to arrive at the place until the hour for the appointment had arrived. On riding along, I began to think on the probable issue of the scene before me, and my mind, at times would misgive me. I had fairly committed myself. "My hand was to the plow and it was too late to look back." I must, therefore, "make a spoon or spoil a horn." As I have said before, the praying part was with me, the greatest stumbling block. As to the discourse itself, if I could pursue the plan I had laid down, I had not much doubt, but I could perform it; as to the psalmody or singing part, I felt full confidence in myself. I therefore determined to introduce the business by singing a pretty lengthy hymn in order to put my blood in complete circulation before I entered on the other parts of the duty, whatever might be the ludicrous appearance of my person. I knew my dress perfectly corresponded with the occasion. I was dressed in a genteel, plain suit of black cloth, of a good quality. I was always opposed to extravagance in dress, when able to wear good clothes. I never was inclined to wear a ruffled shirt, and I seldom wore any kind of gloves, unless in very cold weather and then I chose woolen mittens—boots, I was opposed to wearing, not that I disliked the boot itself, but for two reasons—first, my leg was entirely too small to fill up the boot, and secondly, my leg was placed so exactly in the centre of my foot, that it threw so much of my heel behind, as to make it difficult to draw on a boot that would fit. Necessity has often since compelled me to wear a garment that I disliked, but not so at the time I speak of. I contrived to delay time so as to arrive at the place a little later than the appointment. I found a goodly number of people waiting. I was soon met by Mr. Van Zandt and several others; I delivered Mr. Cunningham's note which was quite satisfactory, and after making a hasty arrangement of my notes, was conducted into the church, I proceeded on the plan that I had purposed and succeded in getting through without much difficulty. When I had concluded speaking I requested one of the brethren to pray, which was readily complied with and after the usual benediction, I sat down in the pulpit to breathe. In the time, the hat went round for contribution, and after I descended, I was presented with sixteen dollars and two bits. I pretended to decline taking so much but after a little urging accepted it with thankfulness. I was then urged to go to dinner and spend the evening but declined on the ground that I was not in the habit of eating dinner; that my health did not admit of it; that I was compelled, if possible, to be at Pendleton Court-house in a given time, and had not a moment to lose. I put put off in all haste and went on my way, rejoicing that I had been so fortunate. Whether this could really be considered any crime, I have never been able to decide with myself, but, as no harm grew out of it to any one, and as it served to relieve my present embarrassment, perhaps I am too willing it should be excused; at all events it rested a profound secret with myself, and until within one year past, I never divulged it to my wife, nor to any friend, knowing if I told it once, I might as well publish it at once. I had almost forgotten it, when one day, not twelve months ago, in looking over some old papers, I came across the old journal which brought it to mind, when I began to laugh and amused my family by relating the circumstance.

I returned again to teaching singing school, as usual. I was still afflicted in an extraordinary way, and had tried the best physicians that I could hear of, but all was in vain, and I began to think of giving over all further efforts, as I had but little faith in magic, as it is called. At length I one day happened in company where there was to be a man who had lived in the neighborhood where I then was. He had gone some fifty or sixty miles lower down the country, where he had married and settled himself. He had come up with his wife on a visit among his friends. In conversation he began to make some strange statements about a negro that lived in his neighborhood. I knew the man was thought to be a man of truth, but still I did not know how to give full credit to his story. He stated among a number of things, that people had come a considerable distance to hear from him about stray horses, stolen property, and a great many other things, and that he had performed many cures, in fact, he made him out a fair prodigy that could tell every thing, and do almost anything. I listened with attention, but asked no questions as the discourse was not directed to me, neither do I suppose that I was thought of as being interested in the subject in any way. I went on and tried the cure. The method of performing it was somewhat similar to the one attempted upon me by Gilbert and his negro, as described in a preceding chapter ; with this exception, that I complied literally with the instructions of the magician, or whatever he might be termed, and however strange it may appear to others, I was entirely cured. For thirty years after, which is at my present writing, I have never been afflicted with a similar disease.

NOTE.—It is certainly a question, too hard to be solved, by short sighted man, to separate the mysterious union that exists between the mind and body, or to render the proper antidote possessing the two fold qualities of relieving both mind and body. The healing art has been a study fraught with more interest than any other in the world, and the investigating mind is still in busy quest, for some catholicon to answer the afflictions of man. Nations differ in their mode, and manner of treating these things—some nations resort to spiritual treatment, some to cunjuration, some to specifics under the character of drugs and medicines. With due respect Moses hung up the image of a Serpent in the tents of the Israelites to cure their maladies ; the Arabians, the Africans, and Indians resort to mysterious and hidden tricks. Other nations as ourselves, confide more in minerals, vegetables, and other appliances, to cure, believing they possess more charms, and greater virtues. but after all, we still grope in the dark, and are bound to confess that " the Lord giveth, and the Lord taketh away, and blessed be the name of the Lord." J. M. R.

CHAPTER XXII.

VISIT TO TENNESSEE.—ENCOUNTER WITH INDIANS.

USELESS would it be to say anything about matters for several years, as nothing of note transpired until the year 1810. In the fall of that year I concluded to remove to the State of Tennessee. There was a considerable pressure in consequence of the late embargo, and money had become scarce, and my affairs as well as that of many others had become somewhat embarrassed. In order to prepare for moving, I had to sell off my property at a very low rate. I made up my mind, however, and determined to move, and to that end concluded to go and see the country. I took my negro along to work for provisions while I should return for my family. For fear of having my negro stolen, I did not pass through the Indian country, but took a circuitous route through the upper part of South Carolina and crossed the mountains at Eastatowe Gap, opposite the head of Frenchbroad; thence down the river, passing Ashville, Newport, Seirsville, Knoxville and Kingston, where I crossed Clinch River, and went down the Tennessee River into the Tennessee valley, twenty-five miles above the Highwassee garrison. It was then a newly settled place. Here I made my choice as being a place to which I felt inclined to move. The lands were all covered by military warrants from North Carolina, and in the hands of speculators, making it very difficult to get good titles. I therefore rented a small farm, of twenty acres, with a small cabin on it. I hired out my negro to work for some corn and wheat, by the time I should return with my family, and prepared to start for home.

I concluded in returning to pass through the Cherokee nation, it being much the nearer way. There were but few places of accommodation, and they were all kept by half breeds, or white men who had intermarried with the Indians. It was necessary that I should use one of my horses to carry provisions and corn ; one was an Indian pony that had been accustomed to it ; I tied his pack on in the morning, fixed his halter, turned him loose, and he followed close up all day. What few stands there were on the road, were a hard day's ride apart; consequently, if you missed the first, you missed them the whole way, unless you rode late in the night. I provided as much provisions for myself and horses as would keep us for twenty-four hours at least. It was late in the morning when I started, and was detained some time at the ferry on the Tennessee river ; this threw me back, so that I missed the first stand by several miles. I made a fire, tied my animals, and encamped by the road side ; I was a stranger to the route and did not even know where the Indians lived who were scattered along it, for the purpose of selling corn, fodder, potatoes, &c., to travellers. I would have preferred camping close to one every night, for if you camp close to an Indian, you are never in danger of getting your property stolen.

On the second day I was detained again at the ferry on the Highwassee River, which compelled me to again camp alone by the rapids. I was rather disagreeably situated. The agency was then sitting and I was not more than six miles from the place, and the Indians were passing me at all hours of the night and many of them were drunk, so that of course I got but little sleep. Fortnnately, I understood a good deal of their lingo and could speak some of it; could ask the names of places, distances, and the prices and names of articles that I wanted, and could answer in the negative or affirmative to any question they would ask me. They are a singular people. If you ask a few words in Indian, they immediately conclude you understand them perfectly, and know a great deal more than perhaps you really do, and are disposed to be much more friendly to you than if they think you do not understand them, and will immediately talk English with you, when otherwise they would not. The Cherokees mostly all understand English; but if there is a hundred by, you can never get but one to talk English to you at the same time. I got corn and fodder plenty for my horses among them. On the fourth day I had to pass through a turnpike, and through a place called Teloney Towns, said to be the worst place in the whole Indian Nation for stealing or robbing. These towns extend along a narrow valley of rich land, on what the Indians called the Talking Rock Creek, between the Coosa River and Long Swamp. They extend four or five miles along the valley, in villages but a short distance apart.

It was late in the morning when I had to pass through these towns, and there was no place to stay at where entertainment could be found among the whites, until I got through the Long Swamp, which was at least twelve miles off. The man that kept the turnpike was an Indian, who was very inquisitive to know how far I intended going that night. Having told him Long Swamp, he told me I could not get there that night with a pack horse, but would have to camp out. I told him that I would have to go, even if forced to ride all night. He shook his head and laughingly replied, I would have to sleep when I had passed through the last town. It was near sunset, and looking forward the straight road, before me, I observed an Indian with his gun on his shoulder, approaching. When he came up, he saluted me with "canaulee," that is, brother, or good friend. My reply was, "oszeruki," mighty good; we shook hands very cordially. I asked him how far it was to Stile's; he signed ten miles. I told him I was in a hurry, and must go there that night. "Enclah!" was his reply; "you must lie down and sleep before you get there." I told him of my hurry, and bid him good bye. After getting ahead, perhaps two or three hundred yards, I turned around on my horse, and saw the fellow standing in the same place, gazing after me. I did not like the sign, being in an Indian country, alone, a stranger to the road, which was thinly inhabited by whites, without any means of defence if attacked; my only weapon was a small double bladed knife, one blade long and perfectly keen, like a dirk. I thought it would be advisable to leave the road that night and camp out of sight, but it being a broken and mountainous country, deemed it best to get into some deep bottom, where I would be concealed from the view of the road. In the dusk of the evening the ground where I was passing seemed to favor my intentions. Upon my left was a high ridge, the road passing along the side of it. I turned short off the road and ascended the hill and descending the other side, entered a deep bottom. I thought I would be perfectly secure and out of sight. It was in the month of November, and the nights were cold and frosty, making it necessary to have some fire. I gathered up some wood and made a fire by the side of an old log; stripped my horses and made them fast, with a couple of good halters, to a sapling near the fire, and fed them with corn; arranged my baggage and seated myself by the fire, being cautious to have but a small one so as to have as little light as possible. I drew out my bread and meat and eat my supper, made my bed and laid down by the fire. I was too uneasy to sleep, and passed my time alternately lying down and setting up until after midnight. The night was a clear, starlight one, and not a sound disturbed the deathlike stillness. I examined my horses, gave them some more corn, and once more tried to sleep. I had plenty of clothing and was not afraid of the cold. Before laying down I stripped off my under coat, vest, shoes and leggings. I soon fell asleep, and must have lain about three hours, when I awoke. My fire was nearly out, and I could hear nothing of my horses. I got up and kindled the fire and looked for my horses, but they were gone; it hardly seemed possible that they had been stolen for I had taken so much trouble to find a secluded spot. They were both well shod and if near could have been heard, owing to the gravelly state of the ground. I listened attentively for some time and heard something about fifty or sixty yards up the hollow. It would walk three or four steps, stop a few moments and then go on again; it walked like a human being but stepped exceedingly light. I roused up the fire so the light would shine some distance, put on my shoes, buttoned up my coat and started to make a circuit around in sight of the fire to listen for my horses. I went along the hill-side, down the hollow, and, the first thing I knew, stumbled right into the road. I turned round and saw that my camp was not more than a hundred yards distant, in plain view. The road had turned round the point of the hill and crossed the hollow just below me. The discovery of this fact forced upon my mind the unpleasant conclusion that my horses had been stolen, and it was vain to seek further for them in the night; my only chance would be to go back to camp and remain till daylight. I had gone about half-way back, and heard a signal given by a fellow hollowing like an owl.

Knowing the Indian note too well to be deceived, I stopped short and stood a minute or two, convinced that my horses were at the place where the signal was given. I heard some one walking, and was confident it was some one left to watch my movements; thinking it might not be safe to go to camp, for in case of an attack, there might be more than one, and if I had to die it should be in the road, so that there should be some sign left. Taking my course hastily up the hill, by the way I had left the road at night, I gained the edge, and stopped suddenly under two or three large trees that stood close together; my coat was long, of a dark brown color, and hard to be seen in the night. There I remained perfectly still; the fellow continued the owl signal, and striking with a club on an old log; he would strike three times, stop awhile, and then repeat. Suddenly there were sounds of footsteps at no great distance, approaching. Standing still without moving, I drew my knife; in opening the long blade, the spring being stiff, it cracked like the cocking of a gun; the footsteps ceased. I determined not to move until he came in feeling distance and then strike with all my power, thinking it would be a serious battle any way; if killed, to take one of them along. He soon made briskly off; after he got some distance, he began to whistle like a deer that was "scared" but was too far off for the other to hear him. By this time, the morning star was up and day breaking; the other fellow still kept up the signal; it seemed to be near the course of the road, into which I stepped, walking in the direction, stopping occasionally to notice behind me. After walking as far as the noise seemed to be it ceased; while standing to listen, the sound of the horses' shoes striking the gravel at a short distance from the road was quite distinct. Day was breaking; at length they came to a hollow, they keeping along on the hill side near it, myself on the opposite side; in this manner they travelled about two miles, when they crossed the hollow to my side, and stopped in a little flat bushy place about sixty or seventy yards from me. Not being light enough to distinguish objects fairly I patiently waited; when it became so, my horses were in sight but no one perceivable near them. They stood near a large poplar tree; in going to them, it was necessary to pass near it; on my approach, when within twenty feet, there stood a large Indian leaning against the tree; he had not discovered me, but as soon as he did, he broke like a quarter horse, to my rejoicing. With all possible speed was the return to my camp; every thing was safe; I resumed my journey.

After riding seven or eight miles, I came to a camp of seven or eight families, all up and very busy in cooking their breakfast; three or four of the families were of my neighborhood, so I halted and took breakfast with them. The late event was to my mind an interposition of Providence in my favor. Perhaps this idea extends farther than most people are willing to admit; they may think as they please on the subject. My bow was drawn at a venture but the shaft was levelled with an unerring eye and guided by an Omnipotent hand. There is a certain destiny appointed to man—that his way is marked out, and he has to travel to the end—that adversity and prosperity spring from the same source, and will come to those for whom they are appointed. As to the future destiny of man, it is not for me to speak, for that point is so much disputed among wise men, that it would be simplicity in me to meddle with it, but it is probable, with my thinking, that the material part of man will remain in this world as long as it is a world. The spirit or immaterial part may be free and permitted to soar beyond the giddiest heights of thought and traverse the illimitable bounds of space, but the animal life of man will remain as long in the world as time lasts. I do not now recollect meeting with any writer that has taken notice of the subject but am inclined to think that the same quality of life and animal vitality belongs to the world from its creation without increasing or diminishing its substance; it is surely one of the essential elements necessary to constitute a world and probably will remain like all others. There is a necessary quantity of heat and cold, light and darkness, fire, air, solids, life, and motion, which constitute a world. These existing facts will remain the same as long as Time shall last.

But to resume. I took leave of my company, proceeded on my way, and on the evening of the sixth day after leaving Tennessee, reached home.

CHAPTER XXIII.

REMOVAL TO TENNESSEE—LAST REMARKS.

ONLY A FEW DAYS elapsed, after my return, before I commenced the preparations necessary for my removal. Some difficulty was experienced; being unable to procure a fair price and but little money, for scarcely any thing. This is commonly the case in such situations. Having to move on pack horses, nothing could be taken but my beds and clothing. I hired a man to go with me and assist me. He had previously been a trader among the Indians, and was acquainted with all their manners and customs, and could speak and understand their language. This was of great use to me for I had all my horse-feed to buy from them; besides, I took some light articles along, which in passing through their country, could be sold at great advantage. We had three children, all small, the oldest being only a few months over four years of age. I carried the two oldest on the same horse, and my wife carried the youngest, while my hired man took it deliberately on foot, and drove the pack-horses. We traveled slow and were detained by bad weather and high waters, but on the 24th of December, arrived on the bank of the Tennessee river, at the Indian Old Fields. We camped for the night, near the river, and in the morning I paid and dismissed my man. I then crossed the river with my baggage and with some trouble got it to a house on the hill, about a mile distant, where we were treated with great hospitality. It was Christmas day and we got a good dinner, the first meal we had taken in a house for fifteen days. After dinner I went out and got some help to get my goods to the place I had rented, which was seven or eight miles off, and next day moved on to it. Here. like beginning the world anew, we found ourselves without an article of furniture, either kitchen or household, and but little money. We were among a new race of people, as it were, who had been mostly raised in the mountains, with different manners and customs, and without much regard for either religion or the Sabbath, making it a day for sporting, hunting, fishing, &c. We were not accustomed to this, and although fond of camping out and hunting, yet I had never done so on Sunday, and always made it rule to observe that day. There were a few families who were exceptions and who would not eat fish which they knew to be caught on Sunday, and would permit a deer or turkey to pass though their yards, on that day, without interruption, even by the dogs. There were a few preachers among them, but they were the most avaricious set there, and would take advantage of a man's necessities sooner than any others; but take the community generally, they were excellent neighbors, and as friendly, hospitable a people as the world affords. I have never been so unfortunate as to have a bad neighbor in my life, and among all the men with whom I have met who would take all advantage in dealing, and cheat me out of my last cent, yet they would act the part of a friendly neighbor.

There was but one tailor in the country, and he was partly above working. I proclaimed myself and was soon crowded with work, and fortunately pleased the people, got good prices and as provisions were low, and brought to me without any trouble, I got along very well. By working day and night I soon got supplied with necessaries for housekeeping, and besides, had my negro in the field preparing for a crop. I soon found that industry was the best recommendation a man could have. My wife was industrious, and being a good weaver and seamstress, went to work also, and we were soon comfortably situated. I soon got a cow or two to give us milk. The season was unfavorable for crops, the drouth being one of the severest I have ever seen, but I made enough to do me. Land titles still being uncertain, I leased a place for two years, and my luck continuing good, I began to acquire property. Before leaving Georgia, I sold my gun, because it was impossible to carry it to Tennessee, but when arrived there I found deer and other game plenty. Almost every man kept a fine rifle and were good marksmen, but few were good hunters. They were careful of, and averse to loaning their guns, but at length I succeeded in borrowing one with a small bore which was thought insufficient to kill deer, but people soon changed their opinions of her. With three of my neighbors who lived in sight and had been very kind to us,—furnishing my family with milk and butter without making any charge,—I always divided my game; neither of them knew how to hunt. I was so fortunate in hunting that people laughingly said I exercised some art to make the deer come to me to be shot down.

It was customary when the first heavy frost fell for the hunters to form small companies, go the mountains and camp until they killed as much meat as they wanted. By this means they had plenty of venison all summer, and often some to sell. The first fall hunt that came on, I went to the head man and petitioned to be one of the party. He laughed and said I could go, but he expected I would get lost, and doubted the sufficiency of my little gun. Agreeing to risk these matters, I accordingly packed up and went. There were four of us, and we went to our place of camping that evening. The next morning each man took his course, agreeing that no one should hunt in the way of the other. When night came I returned having killed one deer, the head hunter one, and the others, nothing. The evening of the second day the head hunter had one, one of the others one, and myself three, and on the third evening the head hunter had one, myself two and the others nothing though they had had as many or more shots than either of us ; but notwithstanding this, the rule of hunting was that each should have an equal share of the meat, while every man kept his own skins. We had now killed ten deer of the largest kind, which we took home, and next day I sold my skins for three dollars apiece.

The next week another party was formed ; one of the men came to me and offered to furnish me with a good rifle, powder and ball, if I would go. We went, and in three days killed thirteen deer and a grissly bear ; six of the deer were of my shooting. This was as much as our horses would pack. In the two hunts my share was twelve good hams, and in the course of the winter I saved about forty-eight good hams. The rest of my venison I divided with my neighbors, who furnished powder and shot in return ; this they done for eight winters. I took one or two hunts in the mountains every winter and one in the summer ; my best hunter would never go there without me. I soon was able to buy me a gun of the best quality.

I was not much inclined to stay in the country, though I believed it to be as good in many respects as any part of the Union. I now live in Louisiana. My wife was opposed to moving, unless her father and mother, who had come to the country, would move also, which was not likely to be the case. Although I pay little attention to dreams, for I am always dreaming, particularly when asleep, I must here mention one, had about this time, which was literally fulfilled. I thought a stranger came to me, that I had never seen ; in conversation, among other things, he urged the propriety of my moving ; I mentioned several obstacles. He said : " You will perhaps have to move at a more unfavorable time ; you are now in a situation to go without much inconvenience, and you had better do so. I still objected. He referred me to the passage in the Bible, where the Angel came to Lot: "Arise and get you out of this place, for the Lord will destroy this city." "So say I unto you," he continued: "Arise, and get you out of this place, or you will have to leave it in a worse condition; pay no attention to your wife's objections; go, while you are able to settle yourself somewhere else." I awoke and while thinking of the singularity of this dream again fell asleep. It was repeated. Next morning I told it to my wife. She said she could easily interpret it: "It is a warning for you to try and get religion, and you had better set about it." In a few days, my wife told her mother the dream. She also interpreted it as a warning to get religion. I thought different, but what I know not, so it passed over and was soon forgotten.

I worked along on the lease I had taken, and was quite fortunate. When it expired, the titles to land having become more safe, I ventured to purchase an excellent farm with about sixty acres open. I put up a comfortable house on it and hired a hand to clear fifteen more acres. I rented out all but twenty acres for three hundred bushels of corn, and sowed ten acres in wheat, keeping the other two to cultivate in corn, off of which I could easily make five hundred bushels or more, for good land generally produced from sixty to ninety bushels to the acre. I have seen a field of two hundred acres on the river measured, average ninety bushels to the acre. I was now so situated as to live without much work, hiring any kind of white labor at from six to eight dollars per month. I began to dabble in public office, such as bailiff, sheriff, etc. I was generally applied to in cases of sales, to act as auctioneer; this of course drew me a great deal from home. I have often thought that I never was unfeeling enough to make a right mean sheriff; never liking to see a poor man distressed and his little property sold for almost nothing; the claimant sometimes unwilling to show lenity and desirous that the officer should collect his debt at any sacrifice. Thus, if he is a man of fine feeling, he has to strain his conscience at times in order to be called a good officer. There were many cases in point in my practice; I will mention but one. There was a poor man in the neighborhood that had a large family; one daughter was grown, the others were mostly small; he had no property only what was in his house, and little enough of that for the use of his family. In order to get some little necessaries he had gone in debt at a small store, for perhaps something over thirty dollars. The old man taught school; his employers were negligent and to urge them would endanger his place. The storekeeper brought suit, obtained judgment, and had an execution issued. He told me he wanted the money collected with all speed. I went with the execution; when the old lady saw me coming, she closed the door against me. I must confess I was not anxious to get in. I went to the claimant and told him he must show property; so he went with me. When we got within sight of the house, he proposed for me to stay back, until he went forward and got in the house; he would sit right in the front door, so that the old lady could not shut it until I got in, for he was determined to have his money if he had to sell the last bed there was in the house. After waiting until I thought he had sufficient time to get in, I rode up. He was sitting in the door talking very religiously to the old lady. She soon saw me coming and ran out to meet me, calling to her daughter to shut the door. She seized me and laughingly said I was such a handsome little man she had long been wanting to hug me and would never have a better opportunity than now. The daughter, to obey the mother's command, gave the door a sudden shove and out came the man and chair into the yard, and at the same time the door was made fast. I begged the old lady to let me go, telling her Mr. B., would tell my wife and perhaps her husband, and it would be apt to make a fuss. But she said she would not let me go so soon, and that Mr. B. need not trouble himself to tell my wife or her husband, for she would tell them both herself, and was sure they would both approve of her conduct.

The storekeeper was a little vexed to think the old lady and her daughter had outwitted him, and that we had to go back as we came, and he took out a *ca. sa.* for the old man's body, but by some means he heard of it and quit his school to keep out of the way. Hearing he was at home I went there after him but found the doors once more closed against me. In a few days, however, some of his employers, in order that they might not be deprived of his services, made arrangements to settle the debt, and so the matter ended.

The position I occupied, rendered me liable to fall into all kinds of company, and it almost became necessary for me to comply with the general rules of society. In those days the people were more on an equality than now; there was less distinction between the rich and the poor, and vastly more familiarity and neighborship among men, as is generally the case in all new countries. There was a class rather below mediocrity, but take the body of the people, they all stood on equal ground when assembled together. The judge, the lawyer, the sheriff, the magistrate and the farmer were all alike. John, Tom, Dick and Toby were familiar styles of salutation amongst them, and in time of court, as soon as the judge descended from the bench there was a room called for, and company invited in, and every one who chose, called in his bottle of whatever kind of liquor he wanted to drink. There was no such thing known as calling for liquor by the glass. Whoever could sing the best song, or tell the best story, was the best fellow. As for myself I could sing almost any kind of a song that might be called for, and tell a great many stories of different kinds, besides was a great mimic, which by the way I think is a great fault, although guilty myself. All was fun and frolic until the hour that we chose to adjourn for bed. There was never any dispute or contention admitted, nor any party question discussed among us in these evening or night frolics.

Those that were disposed to be quarrelsome, formed a separate club by themselves; they generally left town about dusk for some place within two or three miles, that suited them, and where undisturbed, they could riot all night. These Tennesseeans were mostly fond of strong liquor, and could drink a good quantity; neither was it considered disreputable.

I was now in good circumstances, making money easy, if not fast, yet sure, I was clear of debt, and had always corn, wheat, and meat, to sell; I had a wagon and a first rate team; eleven good horses and other property. I then stood at par with the best men in the country. Under these circumstanstances I considered myself settled for life, and was to commence putting up a set of mills, for I was situated on an elegant stream.

Our venerable father wrote the foregoing narrative at the age of seventy-four, in the year 1836, in the State of Louisiana, and was compelled to close, on account of his eyes and nerves failing.

> "How sleep the brave who sink to rest
> By all their country's wishes blest!
> When Spring with dewy fingers cold,
> Returns to deck their hallowed mould,
> She then shall dress a sweeter sod
> Than Fancy's feet have ever trod.
>
> "By fairy hands their knell is rung
> By forms unseen their dirge is sung;
> There Honor comes, a pilgrim gray,
> To bless the turf that wraps their clay
> And Freedom shall awhile repair
> To dwell a weeping hermit there."

THE END.

THE AMERICAN MILITARY EXPERIENCE

Brown, Richard C. **Social Attitudes of American Generals, 1898-1940.** 1979

Erney, Richard Alton. **The Public Life of Henry Dearborn.** 1979

Koistinen, Paul A.C. **The Hammer and the Sword.** 1979

Parrish, Noel Francis. **Behind the Sheltering Bomb.** 1979

Rutman, Darrett Bruce. **A Militant New World, 1607-1640.** 1979

Kohn, Richard H., editor. **Anglo-American Antimilitary Tracts, 1697-1830.** 1979

Kohn, Richard H., editor. **Military Laws of the United States, From the Civil War Through the War Powers Act of 1973.** 1979

Arnold, Isaac N. **The Life of Benedict Arnold.** 1880

Ayres, Leonard P. **The War with Germany.** 1919

Biderman, Albert D. **March to Calumny.** 1963

Chandler, Charles DeForest and Frank P. Lahm. **How our Army Grew Wings.** 1943

Collins, James Potter. **Autobiography of a Revolutionary Soldier.** 1859

Elliott, Charles Winslow. **Winfield Scott.** 1937

Gould, Benjamin Apthorp. **Investigations in the Military and Anthropological Statistics of American Soldiers.** 1869

Grinker, Roy R. and John P. Spiegel. **War Neuroses.** 1945

Hunt, Elvid. **History of Fort Leavenworth, 1827-1927.** 1926

Leahy, William D. **I Was There.** 1950

Lejeune, John A. **The Reminiscences of a Marine.** 1930

Logan, John A. **The Volunteer Soldier of America.** 1887

Long, John D. **The New American Navy.** 1903. Two vols. in one

Meyers, Augustus. **Ten Years in the Ranks U.S. Army.** 1914

Michie, Peter S. **The Life and Letters of Emory Upton.** 1885

Millis, Walter. **The Martial Spirit.** 1931

Mott, T[homas] Bentley. **Twenty Years as Military Attaché.** 1937

Palmer, John McAuley. **America in Arms.** 1941

Pyle, Ernie. **Here is Your War.** 1943

Riker, William H. **Soldiers of the States.** 1957

Roe, Frances M.A. **Army Letters From an Officer's Wife, 1871-1888.** 1909

Shippen, E[dward]. **Thirty Years at Sea.** 1879

Smith, Louis. **American Democracy and Military Power.** 1951

Steiner, Bernard C. **The Life and Correspondence of James McHenry.** 1907

Sylvester, Herbert Milton. **Indian Wars of New England.** 1910. Three vols.

[Totten, Joseph Gilbert]. **Report of General J.G. Totten, Chief Engineer, on the Subject of National Defences.** 1851

Truscott, L[ucian] K., Jr. **Command Missions.** 1954

U.S. Congress. **American State Papers.** 1834/1860/1861. Four vols.

U.S. Congress. **Military Situation in the Far East.** 1951. Five vols.

U.S. Congress. **Organizing for National Security.** 1961. Three vols. in two

[U.S. Bureau of Labor Statistics], U.S. Congress. **Wartime Technological Developments.** 1945. Two vols. in one

U.S. Congress. **Report of the Board on Fortifications or other Defenses Appointed by the President of the United States Under the Provisions of the Act of Congress, Approved March 3, 1885** *and* **Plates to Accompany the Report.** 1886. Two vols. in one

U.S. President's Air Policy Commission. **Survival in the Air Age.** 1948

U.S. Selective Service System. **Backgrounds of Selective Service.** 1947. Two vols. in four

White, Howard. **Executive Influence in Determining Military Policy in the United States.** 1925

Winthrop, William. **Military Law and Precedents.** 1920